He became Chairman of U.T.V. in 1984 and
d Ulster Waterways, the redevelopment of Belfast's
a past President of the Northern Ireland Chamber o
theatre, cinema and golf and is an enthusiastic memb
ncluded Midnight Oil (1961); A Television First
yal County Down – The First 100 Years (1989). B
lin, and spent the early years of his career in newspaper journalism before becoming
He became Chairman of U.T.V. in 1984 and retired in 1990. He has been actively
velopment of Belfast's Laganside and the launch of celebratory historic murals in
rn Ireland Chamber of Commerce and Industry and President of the Association
is an enthusiastic member of the Royal County Down Golf Club and Royal Palm
A Television First (1977); A Musing – on the lighter side of Ulster Televison
st 100 Years (1989). Brumwell Henderson C.B.E., M.A., D.Litt., F.R.T.S.,
of his career in newspaper journalism before becoming Ulster Television's (UTV)
TV in 1984 and retired in 1990. He has been actively involved in projects as diverse
and the launch of celebratory historic murals in Ballynahinch, Co. Down. He has
and Industry and President of the Association of Ulster Drama Festivals. For
Royal County Down Golf Club and Royal Palm Golf Club, Naples, Florida. His
Musing – on the lighter side of Ulster Televison and its first 25 years (1984); and
ll Henderson C.B.E., M.A., D.Litt., F.R.T.S., F.Inst.D., F.C.I.M., was
urnalism before becoming Ulster Television's (UTV) first Managing Director, a
1990. He has been actively involved in projects as diverse as Co-Operation Ireland
ry historic murals in Ballynahinch, Co. Down. He has been, among other things,
t of the Association of Ulster Drama Festivals. For recreation, he enjoys reading,
lub and Royal Palm Golf Club, Naples, Florida. His previous publications have
ide of Ulster Televison and its first 25 years (1984); and (with Harry McCaw)
A., D.Litt., F.R.T.S., F.Inst.D., F.C.I.M., was educated at Trinity College,
ter Television's (UTV) first Managing Director, a position he held from 1959 to
volved in projects as diverse as Co-Operation Ireland and Ulster Waterways, the
ynahinch, Co. Down. He has been, among other things, a past President of the
f Ulster Drama Festivals. For recreation, he enjoys reading, theatre, cinema and
m Golf Club, Naples, Florida. His previous publications have included Midnight
n and its first 25 years (1984); and (with Harry McCaw) Royal County Down
., F.Inst.D., F.C.I.M., was educated at Trinity College, Dublin, and spent the
TV) first Managing Director, a position he held from 1959 to 1983. He became
as diverse as Co-Operation Ireland and Ulster Waterways, the redevelopment of
own. He has been, among other things, a past President of the Northern Ireland
Festivals. For recreation, he enjoys reading, theatre, cinema and golf and is an
aples, Florida. His previous publications have included Midnight Oil (1961); A
25 years (1984); and (with Harry McCaw) Royal County Down – The First
F.R.T.S., F.Inst.D., F.C.I.M., was educated at Trinity College, Dublin, and
eer in newspaper journalism before becoming Ulster Television's (UTV) first
position he held from 1959 to 1983. He became Chairman

Brumwell Hend... F.R.T.S., F.Inst.D., F.C.I... newspaper jou
M.A., D.Litt., F.R.T.S., F.Inst.D., and spent the early years of his career in newspaper jou
Trinity College, Dublin, and spent the early years of his career in newspaper ... a position he held from 1959 t
Ulster Television's (UTV) first Managing Director, a position he held from 1959 ... projects as diverse as Co-Operation Ir
in 1990. He has been actively involved in projects as diverse as Co-Operation ... He has been, among other
celebratory historic murals in Ballynahinch, Co. Down. He has been, among other ... For recreation, he enjoys
President of the Association of Ulster Drama Festivals. For recreation, he enjoys ... His previous publication
Golf Club and Royal Palm Golf Club, Naples, Florida. His previous publications ... (with Harry McCa
lighter side of Ulster Televison and its first 25 years (1984); and (with Harry McCa
M.A., D.Litt., F.R.T.S., F.Inst.D., F.C.I.M., was educated at Trinity Colle
Ulster Television's (UTV) first Managing Director, a position he held from 1959
involved in projects as diverse as Co-Operation Ireland and Ulster Waterways,
Ballynahinch, Co. Down. He has been, among other things, a past President of th
of Ulster Drama Festivals. For recreation, he enjoys reading, theatre, cinema and g
Golf Club, Naples, Florida. His previous publications have included Midnight Oil
and its first 25 years (1984); and (with Harry McCaw) Royal County Down –
F.Inst.D., F.C.I.M., was educated at Trinity College, Dublin, and spent the ear
first Managing Director, a position he held from 1959 to 1983. He became Chairma
as Co-Operation Ireland and Ulster Waterways, the redevelopment of Belfast's La
been, among other things, a past President of the Northern Ireland Chamber of Co
recreation, he enjoys reading, theatre, cinema and golf and is an enthusiastic member
previous publications have included Midnight Oil (1961); A Television First (197
(with Harry McCaw) Royal County Down – The First 100 Years (1989).
educated at Trinity College, Dublin, and spent the early years of his career in news
position he held from 1959 to 1983. He became Chairman of UTV in 1984 and re
and Ulster Waterways, the redevelopment of Belfast's Laganside and the launch of
past President of the Northern Ireland Chamber of Commerce and Industry and
theatre, cinema and golf and is an enthusiastic member of the Royal County Down
included Midnight Oil (1961); A Television First (1977); A Musing – on the
Royal County Down – The First 100 Years (1989). Brumwell Henderson C.B
Dublin, and spent the early years of his career in newspaper journalism before becom
1983. He became Chairman of UTV in 1984 and retired in 1990. He has been ac
redevelopment of Belfast's Laganside and the launch of celebratory historic murals
Northern Ireland Chamber of Commerce and Industry and President of the Asso
golf and is an enthusiastic member of the Royal County Down Golf Club and Ro
Oil (1961); A Television First (1977); A Musing – on the lighter side of Ulster
– The First 100 Years (1989). Brumwell Henderson C.B.E., M.A., D.Litt.,
early years of his career in newspaper journalism before becoming Ulster Televisio
Chairman of UTV in 1984 and retired in 1990. He has been actively involved in
Belfast's Laganside and the launch of celebratory historic murals in Ballynahinch,
Chamber of Commerce and Industry and President of the Association of Ulster
enthusiastic member of the Royal County Down Golf Club and Royal Palm Gol
Television First (1977); A Musing – on the lighter side of Ulster Televison and
... (1989). Brumwell Henderson C.B.E., M.A., ... early years

BRUM

A Life in Television

BRUM
A Life in Television

BRUM HENDERSON

Appletree Press

First published in 2003 by Appletree Press Ltd
The Old Potato Station
14 Howard Street South
Belfast
BT7 1AP

Tel: +44 (0) 28 90 243074
Fax: +44 (0) 28 90 246756
Web Site: www.appletree.ie
E-mail: reception@appletree.ie

Photographs: courtesy of the author. Cover photograph: by Leslie Stuart, courtesy of the author. Image Scanning by Scanhouse UK Ltd., Kinetic Centre, Theobald Street, Borehamwood, Herts., WD6 4PJ. Design, typesetting and copy-editing by Appletree Press Ltd. The Old Potato Station, 14 Howard Street South, Belfast, BT7 1AP. Printed on text paper 80 GSM BPNS and 130 GSM Matt A/P. Printed and bound in India at Gopsons Papers Ltd., Noida.

Brum – A Life in Television

ISBN 0 86281 864 8

A catalogue record for this book is available from the British Library.

Commissioning & General Editor: Paul Harron
Design: Joanne Thompson
Production: Paul McAvoy

9 8 7 6 5 4 3 2 1

Contents

Author's Foreword

Back in 1959 when Ulster Television had been on the air for a month or so I was passing through North Antrim and saw a plume of smoke rising from a whitewashed cottage from which protruded a tall mast on top of which was the new shield aerial required to receive our station's pictures. I tapped on the open door, entered and saw an elderly male figure crouched over a turf fire which was near to a large television set and he was reading the Belfast *News Letter*. I inquired did he enjoy the programmes and he replied: 'They're not half bad – near as good as the radio – but the light's powerful hard to read by'.

Introduction

Television looms so large that it is sometimes hard to believe there was a time when it was new. That was when I became involved. I led Ulster Television when it was seen as a crazy gamble and when I left it life without commercial television was unthinkable. This book tries to recapture the best and worst of it as well as to paint a partial picture of my life away from the box. It is a memoir in the true sense, written entirely from memory; happily the events and people are still vivid. It does not seek comprehensiveness but presents a few highlights which may be interesting or amusing or both. They include many remarkable personalities but the full *dramatis personae* of my life is larger. In seven decades I made a host of good friends and collaborated with outstanding people and professionals but it is simply not possible in this book to identify and to thank them all. They surely know who they are and I hope deeply that they already know the extent of my gratitude. I can but mention only those involved in the book's preparation. Doreen McDowell transcribed my desultorily dictated (at the request of many friends) reminiscences with the same patience and polish she exhibited over many years as my personal assistant at Ulster Television while Brian Cathcart brought his firm talent and skills to bear on the narrative – I am grateful to both. I am also grateful to my publisher and my editor at Appletree Press, Paul Harron, who guided the book to completion, and also to Stratton Mills for his 'legal-eagle' eye. Finally, my gratitude to Pat, Glynis and Sally – whose enrichment of my life beyond these pages is beyond measure – and I crave their indulgence for what might have seemed avoidable absences.

Ballynahinch 2003

1
Lucky Youth

My childhood was an idyll – a small boy's paradise with a lake to sail on, trees to climb and fruit gardens to plunder. A village full of playmates lay just beyond the gate and mischief and adventure beckoned from every field and barn, every lane and wood. I came across people of every kind from hoary countrymen to royalty, and experienced kindness from almost all, while my early education seems like a catalogue of japes and scrapes with a few lessons thrown in by way of ballast. Many of us see our early life in such a rose-tinted light, all blazing summers and snow-white winters, and it is often an illusion. Not for me. Although I grew up against the background of Depression and war and was made strongly aware of both in many, many ways I really was a most fortunate child.

I was born on 28th July 1929, three weeks past my due date, in my mother's bedroom in the private secretary's wing of what was then called Government House and is now known as Hillsborough Castle. Either out of despair that I would ever make my appearance or in the hope that it would encourage me on my way, my mother had resorted to a couple of stiff drinks that day and her reward was a strapping ten pound baby, her second son. She would say later that despite my considerable size the birth was not at all difficult, so perhaps the alcohol helped. For me, I like to think I started life with a drop of Scotch in my veins.

'Brum' comes from Brumwell. I was named after Sir Brumwell Thomas, a friend of the family and the architect of Belfast City Hall as well as many other grand public buildings, most of them in the north of England. He had been given the Belfast commission by my grandfather, Sir James Henderson, Lord Mayor of the city at the time, and the two men later became close. I suspect that something more than friendship lay behind my parents' decision to borrow the name, for Sir Brumwell was a wealthy bachelor and they may have hoped that in due course some of his money might descend upon a young namesake and godson. For me this would have been some small compensation for the burden of a name so easily shortened by schoolboys beyond the friendly 'Brum', but it did not happen, for while the old man had many virtues generosity was not among them. I saw this with my own eyes for I was present once as a schoolboy when he caught a train in Belfast, and saw a porter so outraged by the meanness of the grand old man's tip that he flung the coin on the ground and walked off. Sir Brumwell, quite unabashed, bent down and retrieved it. 'There, young Brum,' he said, 'waste not want not.' Whatever became of his fortune, he did not leave it to me.

Government House in County Down, today the country retreat of Secretaries of State, was in 1929 the official residence of the Duke of Abercorn, first Governor of the fledgling Northern Ireland. My father, formally listed as Commander Oscar Henderson CVO, CBE, DSO, RN (Rtd), had been in the duke's service since 1922, first as private secretary and then as Comptroller in the Governor's household. With that post went a cluster of rooms on the first floor of the house and this apartment was my home for eighteen years. The house itself, built by the Downshires in neo-Georgian style, was quite a place, with its library, its grand dining room to seat thirty people and its Throne Room for ceremonial occasions. Better still – from a small boy's perspective – it stood in a square mile of grounds. Here was the lake, with its island and boat house; here were the abundant trees; here also was a river with bream for catching, a tennis court, a mysterious graveyard and much else besides.

As young children my brother Bill and I were cared for by Nurse, a lovely woman from the north of England whose smile and affection, and occasional firmness, remain fond memories – when eventually she left us to marry a farmer from Cookstown it took me years to forgive her. We also had a cook, Lily Smith, who served my parents for nearly fifty years, and a succession of parlour maids and housemaids. From time to time we even boasted our own butler. We lived, therefore, in some style, but things were not quite as they seemed, for the business of keeping up appearances stretched my father's finances to the limit and beyond.

Historically, the Hendersons had been rich. The family had owned the very profitable Belfast *News Letter* – the oldest newspaper in Britain – for several generations and had long been pillars of the city, playing a leading part in its Victorian development. But much of this wealth was lost through an accident of inheritance (of which more later) and my father, as the third of five sons, was entitled to very little of what remained. Earmarked for a naval career from an early age, he served with distinction in the First World War, notably in the ill-fated Zeebrugge raid of 1918, but post-war disarmament saw him pushed into civilian life long before he wished. Service with the Governor at Hillsborough became a second career, and one that he followed for twenty-five years. His salary was paid on peculiar terms: as Comptroller he received precisely ten per cent of what the Governor was given by Whitehall to maintain his household. This 'tithe' amounted to £800 per annum, a figure that remained unchanged throughout his service. From this my father not only had to fund his own little household of nanny, cook and maids – indispensable to a man of his standing – but he also had to meet the peculiar demands of life as a courtier. These were considerable: to satisfy the imperatives of protocol and of the Governor's social diary, for example, both he and my mother seemed to change their clothes extraordinarily frequently. Four outfits in a day was not uncommon, which meant that they each had to maintain a very large wardrobe, with the attendant costs of cleaning and repair. In fact the salary was not enough, and was supplemented at times by my mother's father, Robert Boyd Henry. (The man who built the Albert Bridge, he was another leading Belfast figure; I inherited from him both the initials R.B.H. and – rather cleverly – some monogrammed silverware.)

None of this ever troubled my brother Bill and me; in fact very little troubled us in those days. Between the village and the house we had quite a gang. There were the head messenger's sons, Stanley and Jackie Agnew; the dentist's sons, Lenny and Brian Meharg; the market gardener's sons, Ronnie and John Malpas; the police sergeant's sons, Ernie and Jackie Wilson, and others. The village was poor in those days – some of today's yuppie homes were then the humblest of dwellings – and we were a democratic bunch. I remember being embarrassed one summer by my sandals, as all the other boys were barefoot, so every morning I took them off and hid them in the hedge. Besides playing cricket and football we fought wars with air guns, catapults and stones, either among ourselves or against the boys of Dromore four miles away. When we were old enough we would cycle everywhere, setting off from home first thing, returning fleetingly for a lunch taken at top speed and then disappearing again for the rest of the day. On Saturdays I had sixpence pocket money which I divided three ways: tuppence for an Aero bar; tuppence for a packet of five Woodbines and tuppence for peppermints to take the smell of smoke off my breath. My parents used to wonder why I had trouble eating lunch those days and the mystery was solved when my father came across the Woodbines. Though he was angry it was not his way to beat his sons so instead he warned me gravely that tobacco would stunt my growth. At the age of eighteen I was six foot four inches tall and reminded him of his warning. He was not amused.

The lake was a special playground. Bill, always resourceful and good with his hands, built a boat of his own, a little top-heavy and easily capsized but dashing enough with its coats of red and black paint. He bought a beautiful anchor for it and one day when we were re-fighting some great sea-battle from history – Bill with his friends in his boat and me with mine in the Governor's dinghy – he used the anchor as a grappling iron. He swung it at the dinghy and it caught hold so I promptly cut the rope and threw it back. It missed, fell in the water, was never retrieved and has lain on my conscience ever since. Another strong memory of the lake is of bathing naked one summer's evening when the Duchess of Abercorn strolled by. This was a very grand lady of whom I was in awe. Sinking instantly to my waist in the water I performed what I hoped would pass for a bow and hoped against hope that she had not noticed my state of undress. She stopped, looked at me, pondered a moment and then called out that it was getting cold and I should come out of the water immediately. I wasn't sure what protocol dictated but I was certain that duchesses and nakedness did not mix. 'No your Grace, it's very warm,' I assured her. 'Nonsense, boy. Now come out,' she replied crossly. Too mortified to comply yet too confused for further speech, I stood transfixed and silent until she lost patience and marched off, declaring: 'You are a disobedient boy and I will tell your father.'

One Easter Sunday – I was eight – Bill and I found our way to the Agricultural Research Institute, a couple of miles from home. My plan was to bring a lamb to our mother, whom I had heard say that she liked to cuddle lambs, but there were none and so we split up to seek our own amusement. While Bill investigated the farm machinery I played in the hay, eventually taking out a box of matches I had in my pocket and striking one to see what would happen. In minutes the place was ablaze and though Bill tried to beat out the flames with his jacket there was nothing to be done. The hay, the barn and, worst of all, an experimental tractor disappeared in the inferno. Duly terrified we returned home, where later a furious father put me in his car and drove me back to the scene to watch the firemen extinguish the last of the embers—he wanted to make sure I understood the enormity of my crime and experienced the fullest possible mortification. Again there were no beatings but I recall a terrible sense of doom and a long talk on the differences between right and wrong. I was also sent to the Institute for a formal dressing-down but, to my father's dismay, the director had no taste for retribution and ended up showing me his stamp collection. Fortunately the bill for the damage, which would have ruined my family, was covered by insurance.

From my tenth year, 1939, we played mainly war games in imitation of the world around us. Though Hillsborough was hardly in the front line, like everywhere else in the United Kingdom it felt the effects of the Second World War. Belfast was eventually bombed – it suffered terrible damage – for the Luftwaffe planes grouped directly above our village before attacking the city and we cowered in the cellars while the engines roared overhead. Security at Government House, normally in the hands of an RUC sergeant, four constables and a few part-time local B Specials, was stepped up in wartime with the addition of a platoon of regular soldiers and the installation of a machine-gun nest on the roof. The Duke and my father set an example by joining the Hillsborough company of the Local Defence Volunteers, a force which, in true *Dad's Army* style, started out with wooden rifles and included men of all ages from 16 to 76. At their first parade the local solicitor called a roll including 'Private the Duke of Abercorn' and 'Private Commander Henderson'. Much later, after they had been renamed the Home Guard and issued with real firearms, there was a tactical exercise and the troop divided into two forces. My father was observing an 'enemy' manoeuvre from behind a tree when a shot rang out and splinters of wood and bark showered upon his head. Though it was supposed to be a blank-round affair one of the B Specials had loaded a live bullet – he explained later that he wanted to 'give a bit of ginger' to the proceedings.

We had rationing, of course, and all the improvisation and skulduggery that went with it. Bill kept hens (though they were pestered mercilessly by the family dog, a Sealyham terrier) and thanks to the local baker we were rarely short of butter. In the heart of County Down, in fact, the supply of food presented few problems but it was different with clothes and my mother and the Duchess, with their special sartorial requirements, felt the loss. On one occasion there was a draper in Lisburn who was prepared to ignore the regulations, and they went to buy what they could. The draper sadly was eventually arrested, fined and ordered to name the customers who were the partners in his crime. Nobly – for it would have caused a scandal – he refused to identify the Governor's wife and my mother but when my father got wind of the affair he was outraged. Besides believing that we at Government House should set an example he was a martinet in such matters. When, for example, we complained about the shallow baths he allowed us he would reply: 'That is what the King and Queen bathe in and if it is good enough for them it is good enough for us.'

Unusually, we were a family who actually knew the King and Queen, or at least we had been presented to them for whenever royalty came to Northern Ireland they stayed at Government House. These visits were always a highlight of life in Hillsborough and my brother and I were directly involved. Every possible assistance was recruited as Government House strove for a few hectic days to replicate something of the grandeur of Buckingham Palace. Friends of my father were brought in as aides-de-camp and the secretaries, constables and B Specials were all given formal parts to play. In rehearsals Bill and I assumed the roles of King and Queen while my father timed every procedure with his stopwatch. The plan was that, no matter how frantic things were below the surface, Northern Ireland would be smooth and well-ordered.

The Prince of Wales, later Edward VIII, was among our visitors. He was serenaded by the band of the local Orange lodge and persuaded to give the Lambeg drum 'a bit of a blatter'. I remember also the stir he caused by 'mitching' from an official function to play a second round at Royal County Down golf club. The Duke of Kent and the beautiful Princess Marina also visited, while the Duke of Gloucester stayed on several occasions. Once in the 1930s he took a fancy to a magnificent Bentley parked outside - the property of one of the aides-de-camp – and after a good dinner decided that he absolutely must take this monster for a spin. Though the hour was late and he was scarcely sober he jumped behind the wheel and roared out through the gate with my father and the car's distressed owner clinging on, begging him to slow down. Fortunately a B Special on the Ballynahinch road, forewarned by telephone, stepped out and brought the car screeching to a halt. 'Why have you stopped me?' the driver called out. 'I am the Duke of Gloucester.' To which, according to my father, the officer replied: 'And I am the King of Siam. You're driving too fast, young man.'

Of all the members of the royal family that we met our undoubted favourite was Queen Elizabeth, later the Queen Mother. As boys our hands would be wet with sweat before an encounter with her husband, King George VI (though in truth he was by no means intimidating), but with her it was quite different. Her eyes always seemed to be just for you and her famous smile enchanted. She visited several times, especially after the war when her brother-in-law, Lord Granville, became Governor, and on those occasions my mother, brother and I were summoned to the library in the evenings to join in games of charades. Her Burlington Bertie was as good as anything I've seen, and she was easily the quickest at recognizing the efforts of others. Meanwhile Dad and Lord Granville tried to pierce the 'Islay Mist'.

The war did nothing to dampen my appetite for mischief; indeed the reverse. We boys (not Bill) lived a life borrowed from the pages of *Just William*. We stole wine from the duke's cellar and cigarettes from my father's study. When it snowed and the hill road froze we waited in the dark for cars slithering their way up, darted out when they neared the top, spun them round and pushed them downward, cheering, before the driver knew what had happened. And as our teens advanced there were other distractions, such as playing pontoon with the soldiers and dallying with the local girls. Dances were held in small halls dotted over the countryside and though they were officially 'dry' we youngsters brought little bottles or 'naggins' in our pockets to liven things up. The entry fee was threepence and the music came from live bands, usually drums, piano and saxophone. The blackout was a great encouragement to courtship, though these were fairly innocent days – those big enough and brave enough to buy a condom at Blake's Surgical Stores in Belfast tended to transfer it, unused, from trouser to trouser as the unsuccessful months slipped by.

Along the way I picked up a little education. After Nurse moved on we acquired a governess, Zena Rankin, who taught me basics in English and French, geography and history, but for some reason no mathematics. Then at nine I was sent to Brackenber, at the time a new and fashionable preparatory school on the Malone Road in Belfast. Apart from a scholarship to Bradfield College I remember it chiefly for two things: the friends I made and the journeys there and back.

Three schoolmates became friends for life and will feature again in this story. They were Paddy Brand, who became one of Belfast's leading retailers, Barry Johnston, a long-serving colleague at Ulster Television, and Randal Kinkead, later my university room-mate. The journeys were long and they showed me a wider life. From Hillsborough I could take the 8 a.m. bus which after many twists and turns would drop me on the Lisburn Road in Belfast, within half a mile of school. Mostly, though, I would cycle to Hillsborough station, take a train to Lisburn, change for Belfast and then board a tram for the last leg. Either way it was a long haul for a small boy, particularly one decked out in red cap, grey suit, red-and-white tie and red-topped socks, which tended to attract unfriendly attention. 'Hey wee lod, are you a wee Prod?' I was asked once by a gang of large youths. I wasn't alone and to my horror my companion answered in kind: 'Hey wee ape, are you a wee Pape?' I ran like the wind. Journeys were also disrupted by bombing but even when there were tedious delays I 'borrowed' a little from my fare allowance to buy sweets.

Because of the war the younger male teachers at Brackenber left to join the services and were replaced by women, notably the Misses Simpson, Jennings and Rankin (my former governess). They were always addressed as 'Sir' although Miss Simpson in particular was in no danger of being mistaken for a man; she was so attractive that most of us fell for her though it was not all romantic. One summer term we rearranged the desks in the classroom so that she had to stand with the sun behind her and her shapely figure showed through her thin summer dresses. Academically she and other teachers served us well showing enterprise and tolerance. I played a 'rude mechanical' in a performance of *A Midsummer Night's Dream* performed against the backdrop of the school air raid shelter. Our 'rude mechanicals' used thick Belfast accents to the dismay of some socially pretentious Malone Road mothers. Other memories include winning the 'best loser' award in a boxing competition and smoking in the scorer's hut during a cricket match (the smoke was apparently visible to all outside but the headmaster merely observed as he passed: 'I hope you lot are not on fire in there.')

A highlight of those years was the waste paper competition – not quite Hitler's downfall, but, to aid the war effort, the city fathers encouraged schools to salvage paper, especially books, and Brackenber rose to the challenge with vigour. My assignment was to scour Hillsborough and its environs on my bicycle, filling basket and panniers with all I could find. After some time, when the calculations were done, it was found that Brackenber had produced the biggest collection per pupil in Belfast. Our reward was a cup and as I was by then head boy I led the delegation to the City Hall to receive our trophy from the hands of the High Sheriff, Tommy Henderson (no relation, but a figure of some interest – he it was who during a speech at Stormont complained that the Catholic Church was 'like an octopus with its testicles all over Ulster'). We carried the cup back to school in the tram, proudly waving it through the window like a team of sporting champions.

In 1943 this idyll was rudely interrupted. Bill, five years older than I, joined the Irish Guards, leaving my mother, who was very close to him, distraught. I, meanwhile, was packed off to Bradfield College, a middling public school in Berkshire, 40 miles west of London, which Bill, my father and my uncle Lilburn had attended before me. Probably Spartan at the best of times, Bradfield in wartime seemed like a prison. To be sent there at fourteen, across the North Channel, leaving all the pleasures of Ulster life behind and hauling suitcase and trunk from ferry to train and from train to bus, seemed an unusual and cruel punishment. Worse still, the day began with a cold shower, supervised by a prefect reclining in a warm bath (occasionally in winter we had to melt the ice in our shower-head with a candle). Bradfield had fagging, so we then had to clean the study, fireplace and shoes of the house prefects. Then we made our beds, polished our shoes and ran half a mile to the dining hall, where breakfast was lumpy porridge, cold toast and jam. My pleas in letters home produced no release but my mother tried to supplement my diet by sending me half a dozen eggs, not one of which completed the journey intact. Furthermore, Bradfield, while cold on showers, was hot on religion: twenty minutes' 'High Church' worship in chapel every morning and twenty more at 'House Prayers' in the evening (with a Plymouth Brethren housemaster); on Sunday ninety minutes in the morning and sixty of Evensong, plus a mid-week evening service of forty-five minutes conducted by the 'Low Church' headmaster, Colonel Hills, a former housemaster at Eton. And in class we studied divinity.

Although boarding school was a shock, the first year – a chilling contrast to Hillsborough days – was the worst and as I learned the ropes and conquered my fears things grew better. The teaching was good and at 14 I passed nine subjects in my School Certificate, albeit by a hair's breadth in mathematics. Specialisation was normal then so I concentrated on French and history. The former was taught by Monsieur Le Grand, a small moustachioed man with a limp acquired in an encounter with a German tank during the First World War. He was known, inevitably, as Froggie. Author of several school textbooks, he was a fine teacher with the gift of communicating a love both for his subject and for his country. Through Froggie, therefore, I first learned of the delights of French literature, poetry and art, although my enduring memory of him is VE Day when, to the accompaniment of the school gramophone, he led us in the *Marseillaise*. His tears of joy were the first I had seen from a grown man.

History, mainly, was the domain of the fearsome John Moulsdale, a sportsman and scholar nicknamed 'Welsher' because (the originality of it!) he came from the Welsh borders. He had a rigid intolerance of those who could do better. As one of these I was required not only to attend regular classes but also to endure special additional 'tuition' in his study in the 'House on the Hill'. There he encouraged concentration by entwining his fingers in my hair and banging my head on his desk. Not surprisingly I lived in terror of this but it had the desired effect: I used to swot up history late into the night, reading by the light from the lavatory outside the dormitory. Only twice did a chink ever show in Moulsdale's steely armour, the first when he said 'Well done' with evident pride after my Higher Certificate results came through and the second when he bade me farewell with the words 'It was good to have known you, Henderson.' I should be grateful to him, particularly for all those extra lessons out of his spare time, but I wish he could have been more humane. Meeting him again years later I saw his kindly core.

Even at Bradfield I indulged my taste for mischief though it was not easy: at the start of term, for example, we had to surrender all our pocket money to the housemaster who doled it out in niggardly quantities. Drinking was therefore difficult, but once in a while we managed to muster enough cash to ride 10 miles to Reading by bicycle and buy pints of beer in a pub. Girls, oddly, were more readily available. There were the young ladies of nearby Downe House, who were our partners in closely-supervised dances once a term; there were the Land Girls, though they were more interested in servicemen or Italian prisoners of war; and there were the school maids, almost all of them Irish. In my final year three of my friends were caught more or less *in flagrante* with maids and expelled, and in the headmaster's subsequent inquiries I too fell under suspicion. I was not, in fact, guilty in the strictest sense, since at the time I was romancing the daughter of the sergeant-major in the Officer Training Corps. This was an alibi I could hardly use, so instead I employed a shameful tactic. 'But sir,' I protested when confronted about the maids, 'they come from the south of Ireland.' The Colonel knew just enough about Ireland to accept this and just too little to see what nonsense it was.

It was a sporting school, though we played soccer rather than rugby, and in time I became a decent full-back. But my preference was for golf and some of us were occasionally allowed to play a round at Calcot, a course near Reading, cycling the 12-mile round trip with our slender bags of clubs on our backs. This was the start of a lifelong love affair with the game. By contrast a 'sport' that left an unwelcome mark on me was boxing. Since I was tall and solid it was always assumed that I would perform well in the ring, even in Brackenber days, although in truth I had little native talent and did not enjoy it. In my final year, therefore, I was matched with another senior boy and by chance landed a punch heavy enough to knock him over. As he fell his head struck a corner post and he suffered a concussion so severe he had to be taken to hospital and it was not known for some time whether he had suffered lasting damage. He was a decent, clever boy who had already won a scholarship to Oxford and the whole affair weighs on my mind.

It would be less than honest to say that I enjoyed Bradfield. Perhaps it taught me independence of spirit and I owe it whatever iron I have in my soul, but I should thank the school for securing my entry to a place that I came to love even more: Trinity College, Dublin.

2
Trinity Lights

Generations of my family went to Trinity so it was a natural choice for me but when the time came there was some hesitation. After those other Hendersons had graduated, Ireland had seen revolution, partition and civil war. The division of the island had further deepened because of Irish neutrality in the Second World War. Dublin seemed farther away and my parents and their friends debated whether I would be better at Oxford, or a continental university, or even on a world tour ('gap year'!). Happily the vote went to Trinity and in 1947 I began an honours degree course in history. On the face of it this was not onerous. Before me lay four years, each broken into three terms just seven weeks in length - 21 weeks a year, plus exams out of term-time in September. With such an undemanding timetable it was not hard to see that this was going to be much different from Bradfield so I resolved to make the most of it. Indeed the academic load was never light enough for me; through most of those four years I attended as few lectures as possible and remained largely a stranger to the Reading Room. My interests lay elsewhere and with no Welsher Moulsdale to bang my head on the desk I gave them free rein.

Home at college was 'rooms'. Rooms in No 9, Front Square were shared, with Randal Kinkead, the son of a mattress manufacturer in Belfast, as my room-mate or 'wife'. Not that the accommodation was luxurious - my parents were horrified when they first saw the filthy wallpaper, peeling paint, the rotting timbers and, worst of all, clear evidence of rats. This was normal for college rooms and if Trinity had not been a venerable institution most of them would have been condemned to be cleared as slums. My father and Uncle James must have pulled some strings and the hovel improved a little and with some second-hand furniture and mattresses from Randal's father we gained a degree of relative 'comfort'. This was sustained for us by our 'skip', or servant, Tracey, who made the beds, cleaned out the fire and emptied the slop buckets (though not necessarily in that order and usually without washing his hands at any stage). He had been in the Royal Navy and approved of me as an officer's son. 'Ulster Fries' were cooked on a solitary gas ring, but every evening except Sunday we had Commons, the obligatory dinner – paid for each term in advance – in the college dining hall. It was plain fare, but solid and hot.

The student body was a curious, happy mixture. Since the college was then still officially 'banned' by the Roman Catholic Church there were relatively few Irish Catholics among the 2,000 undergraduates. The Ulster contingent made up about forty per cent of the student body, and there were also many from England – Trinity was still a popular option for English school-leavers who did not choose Oxford or Cambridge. A number of British ex-servicemen brought an unusual experience of life (and death) to the place, and there were others even more exotic: a Polish prince, the scion of a French champagne family, several Lebanese and Egyptians and a group of sixty Nigerians. These last, a number of whom became my friends, had come to Dublin at the behest of the British Colonial Office with a view to preparing their country for self-government. Sadly, many were killed in the Biafra war of the 1960s. Women students made up a small, lively and welcome minority, though they were not allowed rooms in college and were carefully counted out at the gate at 6 p.m. every evening.

Soon after my arrival I discovered what became my main enthusiasm and occupation for the next four years, the drama society known as Dublin University Players. Randal and I presented ourselves to be auditioned by Barry Roach, a brilliant actor and producer who for some reason never became a professional and we were cast in the annual pantomime. From then on, for four years, Players dominated my life. Looking back, it is easy to see how it became almost a full-time occupation for in those days we had three big productions a year – a pantomime before Christmas, a heavy play in the New Year and a revue in the summer – as well as a handful of one-act plays each term. We also entered the annual drama competition between all the Irish universities including Queen's in Belfast. Most of our productions were staged in a tiny theatre at the top of No 6 in Front Square which seated about fifty, but bigger shows found larger stages at the Royal Irish Academy of Music in Westland Row and even the Peacock Theatre (at the time a try-out theatre for the Abbey). We were always scrabbling for money. Admission to No 6 was threepence – or sixpence including tea and biscuits – and since this income was never enough, every year we topped up the kitty by holding a big fund-raising fancy dress ball at the Metropole Hotel which attracted the best and the worst of Dublin's demi-monde (I recall Brendan Behan as the Pope, standing at the bar tipping back pint after pint.)

The *eminence grise* of Players was R.B.D. French, a lecturer in English and a nephew of Percy French. He had a sharp eye, a sharp wit and a tremendous gift for rhyme and most of our pantomimes, revues and shorter skits flowed from his prolific pen. He kept us in order too, stationing himself in the wings and muttering 'Fluffing my lines! Fluffing my lines!' when we went astray. It was when I was appearing in one of French's pantomimes at the Peacock that I invited Tracey to see the show. The next morning he woke me with the call: 'Time to rise, bare bum.' I was taken aback by this unwonted familiarity until I realized that I had misheard and that this was a compliment on my acting: 'Bare bum' was his version of Beerbohm, as in Beerbohm Tree, the actor.

A few productions linger in the mind. In 1948 in Belfast we won the universities competition with Ibsen's *Master Builder*, although we were nearly lynched when our pianist Anthony Devlin – a staunch Protestant – closed the evening with a jazzed-up version of *God Save the King* – the very unionist audience began ominous mutterings so we fled with our trophies. Another year Glyn Owen's production of *Julius Caesar* in modern dress, with me in the title role, delighted audiences in Dublin and Galway but failed to win the big prize (a judge, Walter Macken, said it would have won if it had been in Irish).

In one of our skits at No 6 the setting was a Hawaiian island and the climax was a volcanic eruption. Over-ambitious, of course and when the moment arrived there was no eruption, not even a 'pop', and the actors had to improvise a limp ending. We had turned to the famous tea and biscuits afterwards when there erupted a mighty bang and a scorched but delighted 'engineer' rushed in shouting: 'I've done it! I've done it!' Another comedy of errors was the work of a fellow Old Bradfieldian who pestered me into giving him the job of assistant stage manager for a light comedy. Rehearsals had had to be held elsewhere but in the theatre itself the actors emerged to find the entire set laid out facing the back of the stage, with the result that the comedy became a farce. When I informed the culprit that he was a stupid fool he produced the wounded reply: 'I'll have you know I'm not as stupid as I look.'

My most successful production involved me in a clash with the college censors. *The Man Who Came to Dinner*, by Moss Hart, was a stylish commercial play which I had long thought perfect for Players but the Trinity. authorities rejected as unsuitable. After years of correspondence permission was grudgingly given 'on condition that the word "bloody" (page 49, line 7) is excised'. The show played to packed audiences at the Academy of Music, with Roach magnificent in the title role and the young Jennifer Johnston in a nice cameo as the weird daughter. The excision became notorious and in the course of the run 'bloody' was replaced with a variety of words until on the last night, to the delight of the audience, it became something beginning with F.

When not involved with Players I spent some of my time on the golf course. By a marvellous tradition members of the university golf club who paid an annual subscription of just £1 had privileges at Royal Dublin Golf Club, where the great Christie O'Connor (Senior) was the professional. Of these privileges I took advantage. My parents worried, inter alia, about my spending so many hours on the course although my uncle James, a Trinity man and a plus two golfer, assured them it would 'do the boy good' to have what he called 'a relief from his studies'. If only he had known. Through golf (of which more later) I made two great friends, Brownlow Pyper, who became Secretary of Trinity after a spell as a salesman with an American floor-covering company, and Roy Hawthorne, much later the chairman of Castlereagh Council. It was Roy who, some time in 1949, introduced me to a Portadown girl who had recently arrived at college. Joy was a dentist's daughter and a medical student, but more to the point so far as I was concerned she was a lively, attractive redhead. Before long we were close. She joined Players and played the lead in a production of Shaw's *You Never Can Tell* which we took successfully to Cheltenham. She also switched to modern languages – medicine was the most demanding course and the change allowed us more time together. It was the beginning of a long relationship.

Trinity is in the heart of Dublin, in easy reach of theatres, cinemas and pubs, and the city and the college at that time shared many characters. One of these was Florence O'Sullivan Donoghue, a flamboyant figure who, at 16, started his student career brilliantly with a Double First and then took it easier. He claimed to be the illegitimate son of an earl, rarely had money and fleeced the tourists trooping in and out of college. Florry wore his hair unfashionably long and would approach Americans asking: 'Spare a penny for a student's haircut?' It was infallible. Another odd figure was Dick Harris who claimed to be related to both Frank and 'Bomber' Harris – an unlikely combination – and though he appeared to be involved in college life and wandered around with a gown over his arm the connection was obscure. One day when degrees were being handed out he appeared in the gown and solemnly processed past the platform clutching a scroll which was a menu from Jammet's, the grand restaurant on Nassau Street. Years later I bumped into Dick and he told me he was in the oil business. Which company, I asked, thinking of Shell or BP. 'Seven Seas cod liver oil,' came the reply. Besides Dick and Florry there was also Eoin 'The Pope' O'Mahony (as he was universally known), a hugely entertaining man with an encyclopaedic knowledge of the Irish aristocracy. He nearly exhausted his own fortune on legal efforts to secure the release of young IRA men such as Brendan Behan who had been imprisoned in Britain before and during the war. This was supposedly why, whenever you met him, the Pope was always after 'a bed or a meal dear boy'.

Of all of them, there was no character larger or more engaging than Behan himself. He was fond of Players and came to most of our productions and camped for a while in my rooms after I evicted 'the Pope'. Behan was working as a housepainter then and had published little, so the benefit of his genius was conferred on his companions. He had a face like the inside of a water melon and a roaring voice which broke readily into oath and song but he was also a kind and sensitive soul with a peculiar regard for the North and Northerners – one of his party tricks, characteristically perverse, was to sing *The Sash My Father Wore* in Irish. My strongest memory of him was in 1948 when I was visiting Paris. I was standing at the corner of the Boulevard Saint Michel when I heard a wild cry of 'How are ye Brum, ye old fuck pig?' and there he was, weaving his way up and clamping me in his odoriferous embrace. 'What are you doing in Paris, Brendan?' I asked, uncomfortably aware that many of those seated in the café terrace behind me were Americans who had understood his greeting perfectly well. 'Drinking and fucking,' he replied at the top of his voice. 'What else is there to do?' It was the start of a raucous holiday together, trawling the bars of the city for conversation and company, ending with a wild 21st birthday party for a friend, Charles Sweeting, who was also in Paris with a few Trinity mates. At one stage in the evening I had to intervene when Brendan tried to pick a fight in the street with a man I recognized as Marcel Cerdan, the world welterweight boxing champion of the time. He capped the occasion by diving naked into the Seine, to the acute displeasure of the gendarmerie. Life was never dull with Brendan.

Money was a problem. My Higher Certificate results at Bradfield had been good enough for a county scholarship but these awards were means tested and my father was just £5 above the line so the cost of my tuition, Commons and rooms was met out of his pocket. Beyond that I had to raise funds myself. Among other things I found the job of writing the 'University Notes' about Trinity life for the *Irish Times*. In exchange for 500 words of news and gossip a week I was paid the sum of £1 which was good money. I had no trouble writing the column, but the same could not be said for the typesetters who had to decipher my writing – poor Charles Sweeting found himself identified in print one week as 'Charles Sheeting' and when I included a correction the following week the name appeared as 'Charles Sweating'. Besides this weekly pound from journalism I topped up my income by playing poker, at which I was lucky, and there was always the last resort: cleaning the Dublin buses in the small hours of the night. It was hard work, but it paid. Capping all this, in my final year I received a happy legacy from my grandmother – enough to buy a bottle-green Morris Minor, the envy of all my contemporaries.

There was little time for academic studies in my busy Bohemian schedule but I did not neglect them entirely. Exams were passed by last-minute cramming – sixteen hours a day for a fortnight or so to make up for all the missed lectures and neglected reading. Desperate measures were sometimes required. I once turned over an exam paper to find only one subject I recognized – the South Sea Bubble – and even on that my knowledge was so sketchy that I didn't know its date. So I slipped a note to my neighbour, a Nigerian called Azikwe, and he passed back the answer: 1720. Unfortunately this exchange was spotted by the invigilator, who informed me with contempt that he would not throw me out of the exam because on the evidence of the note I was so ignorant I was doomed to fail anyway. Happily he was wrong.

It is a useful knack to pick up information quickly and efficiently and I could usually reproduce it plausibly, but, despite the many distractions, I did have a genuine interest in my subject and my memories of the history staff at Trinity are clear. The professor was Theodore W. Moody, a Belfast man of ominous appearance but kindly, even timid nature, and he was assisted by two formidable women. Jocelyn Otway-Ruthven, the lecturer in constitutional history, had a rather poor opinion of me, but Constantia Maxwell, the economic historian who gave me 87 out of 100 for that South Sea Bubble essay, was more generous. The 'court jester' was R.B. McDowell, an amazing Belfast man who is worth a book on his own. A brilliant and original thinker whose lectures were delivered at machine-gun speed, he maintained a shambolic appearance, was indifferent to food but had a huge capacity for port. So single-minded was he about his work, and so oblivious of his surroundings, that he was forever being locked into libraries overnight after failing to notice the closing bell. And once, when he asked me back to his rooms after a debate at the Hist, I had a glimpse of his unusual personal habits. He had attended the Hist in the required white tie and tails but I watched bemused as he peeled these off to reveal underneath the threadbare shirt, tie and waistcoat of his everyday outfit. He had simply put one on over the other and thought this perfectly normal.

From these able people I learned my history and it is a tribute to them as much as to some last-minute exertions that at the end of four extremely happy years at Trinity I not only got an honours degree but narrowly missed a first. Moody in particular taught me lessons that endured: Irish history is a minefield but his detached approach enabled us to absorb a balanced picture even from the most biased or emotional accounts. It is revealing that a young man such as I was, brought up in the North, sent to an English public school and then taught at university by Protestant members of the Anglo-Irish tradition, should have emerged with the political views I then had: more Green than Orange and a good deal more Red than Blue. In many ways this sceptical but even-handed education was a good preparation for what was to come.

Careers were never much on my mind but the approach of finals gave the matter a certain urgency. Journalism was a possibility. I had dabbled in writing with the *Irish Times* and even done a spell as a trainee sub-editor there, witnessing the prodigious quantities of stout that the 'subs' drank in the Pearl Bar to prepare themselves for an evening shift. Ink was in my blood, too, thanks to the Henderson ownership of the *News Letter*. But somehow at this stage it did not attract me. The theatre had magnetic pull, for though I knew I would never be a great actor I yearned to be a producer. It was a huge excitement to be summoned to an audition with the great Michael McLiammoir who, with his partner Hilton Edwards, was a long-time supporter of Players and had followed my career there. To my delight he offered me a job at the Gate Theatre but when it came to money he said he could pay only £2 a week, well short of a living wage. Seeing my face fall he turned on the legendary charm, explaining what a great opportunity this was for me and reminding me in passing that of course Orson Welles had made his start in just such a way at the Gate. At the crucial moment Hilton Edwards appeared and on being told I was unhappy about the money exclaimed: 'Two pounds! That's far too much! That (me!) is only worth a pound a week.' McLiammoir rose to my defence and an argument began, soon interrupted by the third figure in the Gate triumvirate, Lord Longford, chairman of the theatre. Establishing what it was that was agitating the 'old buggers', as he called them, he brought things down to earth with a grim account of the Gate's finances, concluding that bankruptcy would ensue if I was taken on at any price, but that if it must happen they should compromise on twenty-five shillings. Realizing it was hopeless I explained that I could not exist on such an income and left, the shameless McLiammoir hissing after me: 'Remember Orson!' Instead I started on a law degree but when that proved too boring to bear I turned to journalism and to the *News Letter*.

3

The Old Lady of Donegall Street

It was in 1737 that a merchant by the name of Francis Joy produced the first edition of *The Belfast News-Letter and General Advertiser* catering to the 7,000 or so citizens of a town even then showing signs of prosperity to come. Joy was in the paper trade and presumably came to publishing with the idea of finding an additional use for his product; it proved a far-seeing move for his little newspaper took off. After a few years he passed the running of it to his sons, Henry and Robert, and devoted his own attention full-time to the paper manufacturing business. The old man lived to the extraordinary age, for the time, of 93 – long enough to see the *News Letter* firmly established (and incidentally to see the stripling London *Times* launched in 1785), but perhaps fortunately not quite long enough to read news of the execution of his own grandson, Henry Joy McCracken, after the rebellion of 1798. By that date the paper had passed out of the Joys' ownership into the hands of a syndicate of Scottish investors led by one Alexander Mackay, an ancestor of mine. Mackay soon took complete control and in time brought his son and namesake into the firm, but the younger man died before his father and when Alexander senior followed him to the grave in 1844 the paper was left in the hands of his widow and three daughters. Enter now the Hendersons.

The widow Mackay, needing somebody to run the business for her, made an appeal to a former *News Letter* journalist who had left to set up his own paper in Newry, the *Newry Telegraph*. This was James Henderson. He was reluctant to return because his own business was doing well, so he sent his son, James Alexander Henderson, to Belfast in his place. James Alexander was just 21 years old but in short order he injected a new dynamism into the paper, married the middle Mackay daughter and acquired sole ownership of the company.

My family name, therefore, has been linked to the *News Letter* since 1844, while the blood connection - through that Mackay daughter - goes back to 1795.

James Alexander Henderson was a newspaperman through and through with a good instinct for public taste, a willingness to invest in technology and a canny nose for opportunities, and under his guidance the paper became highly profitable. Belfast, too, was growing apace and entering its glory years of the later 19th century. With its great industries and wealth and its booming population it made a tremendous market for an enterprising newspaper. James Alexander was succeeded by his son, James Henderson, an equally able manager who finished his days as Sir James. This was my grandfather. Both men played their parts not only in the business but also in the politics of Belfast, by the end of the Victorian age one of the leading industrial cities of the Empire. James Alexander had been twice Mayor and his son was its first Lord Mayor. Their politics were Unionist and Sir James was a leading light in the anti-Home Rule cause in the early years of the last century. The Hendersons, in short, were among the leaders of Belfast life in the city's heyday.

The death of Sir James in 1914, however, marked the beginning of the calamity in the family's fortunes to which I have already alluded. He had two brothers, Trevor and Charles (Trevor was also knighted), who ran the paper until the late 1920s, and there was also a sister, Florence. It was Florence who lived longest and—perhaps oddly considering that Sir James had six children—as her brothers died one by one much of the family wealth became concentrated in her hands. This was no trifling matter. By the early 1930s the old lady owned the family mansion at Norwood Tower in East Belfast as well as the silver, the glass, the paintings and all the other trappings of a century of success. Above all, she was a large shareholder in the *News Letter*, the fount of this prosperity. All of this, every jot and tittle, she eventually bequeathed not to her own family but to one Sir Christopher Musgrave, a married gentleman and distant relative who had shared many an afternoon tea with the old lady at Norwood. The shock and outrage of the Hendersons was beyond measure and for many years the name of Musgrave was hated in our household but the family did not just sit back and feel sorry for themselves. The brave decision was taken to buy back the newspaper whatever the cost. A large sum of money was raised through the Bank of Ireland; the deal was done and a new generation of Hendersons set about the monumental task of clearing the debt.

Leading this enterprise was my Uncle James, the second son of old Sir James (whose first son, David, had died young). Though Uncle James was undoubtedly the boss he shared the burden of management with his younger brother, concerning himself mostly with the editorial side. Uncle Lilburn, who was one of Northern Ireland's great raconteurs, was responsible for the commercial side while my father, Oscar Henderson, eventually left Government House in 1947 and took charge of the bricks and mortar, plant and works of the *News Letter*. Then they were joined by my brother Bill, who wisely understudied all of them and was destined in time to assume overall control.

So it was a company inseparable from my family's history over the preceding century and a half that the young Brumwell Henderson entered somewhat gingerly late in 1951. Four generations had preceded me, and four Hendersons were already running the place when I arrived. This was an onerous inheritance. I soon learned that it was not Uncle James's way to featherbed his young relatives. After a stiff interview I was offered a pittance of a salary and despatched to the composing room to be taught how to set type by hand, the idea being that I should learn the newspaper trade from the bottom up, the hard way if possible. So that morning I was taken in hand by the overseer, who produced my grandfather's silver composing stick, deftly assembled a couple of words from a font of type (reading backwards of course), tightened it into a forme, pulled a proof and, lo and behold, there, neat, beautiful and the right way around, was his name, Bertie Martin. With that he handed the stick to me, told me to make up my own name in type and take my time about it so that I would get it right. Needless to say it was not as easy as it looked and after what seemed like hours Martin returned to find me near despair.

Somehow those Trinity years of golf, play-acting and poker had not prepared me for this. He glanced at my efforts and said with a chuckle: 'Your uncle told me that would take the kinks out of you.' To calm my panic he shared his 'piece' with me and we had a congenial cup of tea. Then he introduced me to the Linotype machine. This did the same job of making up type but mechanically: type in the script and out came lines of lead type ready for the page. It was tolerably easy to manage for anyone familiar with typewriters who proceeded with caution – the lead, after all, was drawn from a vat of molten metal situated just above head height. If, for example, the change lever was pulled at the wrong moment, boiling liquid lead could squirt out at ear level and hit the wall behind with a splat. Needless to say I accomplished this feat almost immediately, giving myself a dreadful fright but delighting the watching compositors so much that they rose to their feet and applauded. From such humiliations caution and respect are learned.

My grounding in the trade continued with spells in page make-up, stereotyping and the press hall, where we pushed around the reels of newsprint, like huge rolls of lavatory paper taller than a man. Eventually I was given permission one evening to press the button to start the great Vickers printing press, the pride of the paper, purchased with some courage by my father and Uncle Lilburn. From this vast machine poured, neatly folded and warm, the following morning's *News Letter*s – a stirring sight and smell. In my interview Uncle James had told me that newspapers were not an art but a craft and that, while the artist rarely knows satisfaction, the craftsman can experience real fulfilment and pride on seeing the fruit of his labour.

Once I had acquired some familiarity with the business – enough, at least, not to make a fool of myself – I was sent away to be trained properly, doing spells at some of the great British papers of the day. First I was a trainee on the *Glasgow Herald*, alongside a bright young fellow called Alastair Burnet. There we did regular stints through each day in the various departments, moving rapidly from one to another, an approach which had the virtue of giving us a grandstand view of the daily operation of the paper as a whole. Work began in the general manager's office, where a Mr Ewing timed my arrival on his gold watch – I had to be there at 8 a.m. at the latest. He and I would sort the senior executives' mail – Ewing actually read it too – before laying it out in the boardroom where the paper's managers would start their day in informal conversation over coffee (an admirable arrangement which I copied much later). Later in the morning I would shadow the formidable advertising director, Allan Stephen, who combined veiled salesmanship with genial hospitality. His long, liquid lunches were the best nourishment I had in those days. From there I moved on to the sub-editors' room to learn one of the most important and today least regarded skills of the trade. Papers were thin in those days – very thin by modern standards – and there was great pressure for compactness. Unnecessary words meant wasted space so we learned a healthy economy as we squeezed the best of Reuters, the Associated Press, the Press Association, *Times* special services and local news into our eight to ten broadsheet pages. The *Herald*'s chief sub-editor was 'Andy' Anderson, a tough man who after a rigorous night of work would down his pencil, hand over to his deputy and hasten us off to the Glasgow Press Club for several hours of stiff drinking. If we include these nocturnal formalities it was an eighteen-hour day for the trainee and when eventually I returned to Belfast I was a stone lighter.

After Glasgow it was Liverpool, where the process was repeated at the *Daily Post*. There I was given more real work although my journalistic prowess was not what most impressed the paper's owner, Sir Alick Jeans. At the end of my stint he entertained me to dinner at his home and then wrote to my uncle: 'Your nephew has great potential. He also has a remarkable capacity for liquor.' In the eyes of James Henderson, a near teetotaller, this did not constitute praise. After Liverpool came London, with short spells at the Press Association, Reuters, the *Daily Mail* and the *News of the World* – the last of these being the most tightly-run of all, with sub-editors, themselves in suits, all having every item of their work checked by lawyers in black short coats and striped trousers. These were heady days in Fleet Street, when television was not yet competing for advertising, money was no problem and great reporting and writing seemed to thrive amidst a sea of alcohol and a haze of expensive tobacco smoke.

And so, eventually, back to Belfast and my first real job on the family paper. This was in the subs' room, working from 7 p.m. to 4 a.m., six nights a week, with a fortnight's holiday and a wage of £7. Since I was by now engaged to marry my college girlfriend Joy this arrangement had many disadvantages, and it seemed at first a form of banishment from normal life. In fact, as I now see, the disadvantages fell largely on my fiancée, while for me a routine took shape about which few young men would complain. I could rise at 11 a.m., have brunch, play eighteen holes of golf and take in a movie before I had to report for duty at the paper. To cap it all I had the use of a tiny Ford (the Morris had long gone) from the company fleet – a perk I did not appreciate as much as I should have. The work itself, moreover, was made agreeable by the company of my colleagues. The chief sub was David Anderson who, though he could not tolerate sloppiness, was a kindly soul. His deputy was a fierce Derryman called John Rooks, and others on the subbing strength included Billy Warren, formerly of the *Daily Express;* Kenneth Withers, later editor of the paper and at that time the Northern Ireland 'stringer' for the *Times;* and Peter Rea, who handled sports. Most colourful of all was Wilfred McNeilly, a man full of surprises who eventually gave up journalism to write novels.

Joy and I married in 1953, overcoming some concern on both sides of the family that we were too young and that I was not yet well enough established – I believe my wage by then had scaled the heights of £8 per week. We managed, none the less, to buy for £300 a tiny, four-roomed house on the Malone Road, thus attaining a certain threadbare respectability. In 1955 Glynis was born, named after the actress Glynis Johns, and by then we had a very cozy menage, complete with cat as well as baby.

I spent several years in the subs' room before being promoted to the grand-sounding but somewhat deceptive position of assistant editor. This vacancy had arisen because four delightful but very elderly gentlemen who had been subbing specialist features had finally been persuaded to retire and make way for some new blood – me. The hours were more congenial, which suited me in my new role as a father, but the work was less enthralling; mostly these columns seemed to run themselves and my own interventions didn't always help. One column, written by an academic clergyman, always arrived in an almost hieroglyphic script rendered more spectacular by the use of various colours of ink. Although the compositors had no trouble with this I was at a loss to decipher it. Diffidently, I asked the author to write double-spaced with wide margins and he obliged, but the result was a sudden and drastic increase in the number of typographical errors that appeared in print. Thus it was that I discovered that bad handwriting, by forcing people to make the effort to understand, can sometimes be more effective than good – an argument I have deployed in my own defence many times.

Although newspapers are a here-today-gone-tomorrow affair, errors matter. Spelling mistakes and bad grammar reflect on the seriousness and quality of the whole enterprise and it is a foolish newspaperman who imagines that readers do not notice or care. Uncle James made no such mistake. The day would often begin with a series of acid notes from his office complaining about errors big and small, all intended to send the firm message that he sought perfection and nothing less. It was his practice to lunch at the Ulster Club and there the paper would come under further scrutiny as fellow-members drew his attention to mistakes and misjudgments. These could put him in a black mood and on his return somebody had to take the brunt of his anger. It soon became a significant part of my job as assistant editor to be that somebody. I was also given the task of driving the old man home at the end of the day and I learned then that the stern disciplinarian, so admired for his high standards and integrity, had another side. A bachelor, he lived alone, looked after by two devoted servants. The lawns of his house were superior to any of the golfing greens he had played for so many years, but at the age of 60 he gave up the game forever. In his prime he had been a plus two golfer and though his standard slipped only a little with age he announced that he was 'no good any more' and sold his clubs. Instead he took up the piano and spent his evenings in the company of his music and the books he called his 'silent friends'. He was a lonely man, wholly devoted to his newspaper.

Belfast in those days supported no fewer than four daily titles: the *News Letter*, the *Northern Whig*, the *Belfast Telegraph* (in the evening) and the *Irish News*. In addition, three morning papers arrived every day from Dublin and six from London. It was a highly competitive environment and the Belfast papers did not regard themselves as parochial or local in any way. At the *News Letter* we covered international and British news with all the vigour we could muster and we were able to run very late editions of the paper to accommodate late-breaking stories from wherever they came. I was duty editor on the paper at 3 a.m. on the night in March 1953 when news came through that Josef Stalin had died and even at that hour I was able to add two pages of coverage to the final edition, one of them composed entirely of photographs – a feat which few papers, national or regional, could manage today. (As it happens I was almost sacked for my pains because whatever extra sales we made failed by some margin to cover the extra cost in paper and production. Another lesson.)

We remained, of course, a Unionist paper, in some ways close to the Northern Ireland establishment. My brother Bill was a Unionist MP at Stormont for a while, indeed it fell to me to conceal some of his absences from Uncle James, who had reluctantly agreed to the arrangement on the understanding that it would not affect Bill's work. James himself was close with the powers that be – his regular companions at those lunches in the Ulster Club, for example, were Lord Rathcavan, Speaker of the Stormont House of Commons, and Sir William Scott, head of the Northern Ireland civil service. Despite these friendships, the *News Letter* was often critical of the Stormont government and never in its pocket. I saw this at first hand when I became involved in a story about the treatment of mentally ill children.

This was a difficult subject, rarely broached during the fastidious 1950s, but I was privately alerted to a tragic situation by the Town Clerk of Bangor, Terry Graham, and a farming friend of his, David Ewart. They were concerned about the standard of care in County Down and especially the poor quality of management. Graham told me that things were so chaotic that no fewer than 100 children had effectively been 'lost' and were unaccounted for. After checking the details I wrote a tough leader-page article denouncing this state of affairs. The Stormont government was shocked to find itself attacked in this way and the Minister for Health and Local Government, Dame Dehra Parker, summoned my uncle James to her office to account for himself. He stayed where he was, replying coolly that if she wanted to see him his door at the paper was open. The ministerial car duly swept up and the angry Dame was taken by the slow route through the building to his office where, to her further outrage, she found the red 'engaged' light on. When he felt she had waited long enough Uncle James switched to green and spared her five minutes of his time firmly declaring that she should be tackling the problems revealed in the article and not the newspaper which reported them. Then he saw her to her car. It is the only occasion I ever remember when the Stormont government tried to meddle directly in the paper's policy and it was dismissed with admirable firmness.

My own life at the *News Letter* was acquiring new dimensions. I am still proud of the one-off supplements and tabloids I introduced to mark various big events, national and local. One in particular covered the birth of the new town of Newtownabbey. Like most of the others it proved fruitful in attracting advertising and winning goodwill and I like to think that the content, written by an able if unconventional reporter called Norman Ballantine, had editorial merit too. Another notion of mine was to introduce a light-hearted editorial to the paper, along the lines of the famous third leaders in the *Times*. Naturally I was rewarded with the job of writing them, which was heaven if the idea came and hell if it did not. I was also by now reviewing books, though I will admit that this was more of a racket than a high-minded literary pursuit. Books fell into my nebulous domain as assistant editor and I was delighted to discover that I could order as many titles as I liked from the publishers, no matter how fleetingly they were to be mentioned in print. These, once their contents had been skimmed, I could promptly sell on to a book dealer in London who paid me half the cover price plus postage. Better still, I found that the most expensive books were those with pictures and relatively few words; they took even less time to review and 'earned' me more money. As Uncle James remained a parsimonious employer, this was an essential supplement to my income.

By the late 1950s it seemed that I had found my niche and that the course of my life to come was pretty well settled. I was not yet 30 years old, married with two young daughters and a £1,200 house – the arrival of little Sally in 1958 prompted a move to bigger accommodation near the slightly less salubrious Lisburn Road. At work my brother Bill, five years my senior, was clearly destined to succeed Uncle James in due course as the head of the enterprise and I assumed that I would eventually slot in alongside him just as my father had fitted in with his brothers. The *News Letter*, for so long the domain of the Hendersons, would be my life, while by the look of things my responsibilities on the paper would remain primarily editorial.

Then one day in the autumn of 1958 I took a telephone call from Paddy Falloon, whom I had met at some mildly Bohemian evenings in Belfast. Paddy was an hotelier, owner among other properties of the Crawfordsburn Inn. He was also a great lover of people and new ideas and, like me, he went to such gatherings in pursuit of a more exciting Ulster. We had talked and I had liked him. Now he rang to invite me to a gathering of businessmen who wanted to set up a commercial television company serving Northern Ireland. It was the call that changed my life.

4

Job of a Lifetime

The idea that the *News Letter* should have a leading role in a local commercial television company had been around for more than a year. My father had been one of the first people to broach it and he had visited London to discuss it personally with Sir Robert Fraser, the director-general of the Independent Television Authority (ITA), the body set up to regulate the various companies that comprised ITV. He also met Norman Collins of Associated Television (ATV), one of the four big commercial companies which had been operating in England since 1955, seeking advice on an appropriate consortium. My brother Bill and I also had many talks about television and we were encouraged in this by Roy Thomson, the owner of the *Scotsman*, at a meeting of the Young Newspapermen's Association in Edinburgh in 1956. Thomson was forming his own group for a bid in Scotland – not without difficulty, although he was to be successful – and he warned us not to miss the boat. But there was a problem, and it lay with Uncle James, the chairman of the *News Letter*, who disliked broadcasting in all its forms. This distaste could be comical – back in the 1930s he famously warned a *News Letter* man who left to join BBC radio that 'it will never last, you know' – but it was also visceral. So when it came to commercial television he wanted nothing to do with it.

To be fair, from a business point of view this was in many respects prudent. Northern Ireland, with 1.5 million inhabitants, was at this time the smallest region in the United Kingdom to be considered for its own ITV service and there were real doubts about whether it could sustain a commercial station. Only 45,000 homes had television sets, which on the face of it was a pitifully small advertising market – and in commercial broadcasting advertising is all. The local ad industry, too, was tiny: just four agencies had offices in Belfast, with a total staff between them of about 10 people. It was clear that if a station were to have any hope of success the local television and business cultures would both have to undergo a small revolution and, though the ITA was keen to test the waters, the wise heads were shaking gloomily. It was true that across the water the bigger ITV companies were beginning to show profits by 1958, but even they had had enormous difficulties getting started, despite their far larger audiences. They recorded shocking losses in their early years, running into many millions of pounds, and in one case, Associated-Rediffusion, senior directors and managers had to re-mortgage their homes to keep the show on the road. If Uncle James needed commercial arguments to give television a wide berth there were plenty to hand.

Good new businesses, nevertheless, rarely have their origins in prudence and Northern Ireland is rarely short of entrepreneurs prepared to take a risk. Already by the time I received that call from Paddy Falloon one other group had taken shape and had the basis of a solid bid for the contract. Chaired by the Duke of Abercorn (the son of my father's old boss), it included George Lodge, owner of the Grand Opera House, the Hippodrome and various other places of entertainment in Belfast, and the Cunningham family, long-time proprietors of the *Northern Whig* newspaper. These men clearly thought the gamble worthwhile. The emerging group that Paddy spoke for was different in character. It was dominated by Northern Ireland Trailers, a dynamic local company which had grown through its pioneering use of containers at the port of Larne. Its chairman was George MacKean and he was backed by other leading Trailers shareholders: Courtney Catherwood, prominent in the building industry; Ivan Pollin, a Belfast solicitor; and Joe Potter, a leading figure in the motor trade. With them came a second group whose leading light was the Ulster-born film producer William MacQuitty, then basking in the success of his Titanic film *A Night To Remember*. William had been persuaded of the attractions of commercial television by his neighbour in London, Sydney Box, the former head of Gainsborough Pictures and a director of Tyne Tees Television.

Sydney's sister, Betty Box, producer of the successful *Doctor in the House* and its sequels, had been recruited, as had Sir Laurence Olivier. It was William MacQuitty who had initiated the consortium, and his barrister brother James was working 'on the ground' in Northern Ireland to attract support. Together the MacQuittys, the Boxes and Olivier became known as the London group. And besides the London group and the Trailers people there was a third component drawn from the local landowning aristocracy: Lords Antrim, O'Neill and Dunleath. It seemed impressive.

The selection of a winner was not simple. The ITA was running a beauty contest and as in all such affairs the contestants would be viewed from many angles and in a variety of costumes, and they would also be required to give an account of their backgrounds and explain their hopes and plans for the future. In short, the public interest, as well as financial viability, had to be considered. The winning consortium would thus need to look and sound good from every point of view and the group Paddy Falloon spoke for was aware that it lacked certain attributes. While the Duke of Abercorn's partners included strong local newspaper and entertainment elements – these had been the basis of successful bids elsewhere – theirs did not, and this was a 'must' for the ITA. Hence Paddy's call to me. He told me frankly that he had been charged to make 'one last bid' to secure the backing of the *News Letter*.

I was keen and I knew my father and brother were still interested but I was also sure that Uncle James was so implacably opposed that not only would he refuse to allow *News Letter* money to be invested but he would also take it as a personal slight if other members of the family became involved on their own account. It was a difficult moment; Uncle James had been good to me in his gruff and parsimonious way and was probably friendlier towards me than towards the others, but I felt he was wrong about commercial television. My view was that it would come whether we liked it or not and that this was a good business opportunity. In particular I believed that all the pessimism about advertising revenues was misplaced since local television would attract new advertisers who had not previously used print. Nevertheless when Falloon had said his piece my first comment was that Uncle James would never change his mind, to which he responded by asking me to join on a personal basis – I could write, he said, and they needed somebody to do some writing. I thought about this and then replied that I would only come to a meeting if my father and Bill were also invited. In the event it was Bill and I who attended the meeting the following Saturday morning at the headquarters of Northern Ireland Trailers in the Limestone Road, although my father was also present in spirit. For me it was the first of many such meetings in a very, very busy autumn.

The faces around the table were familiar. James MacQuitty and the aristocrats were well known in Northern Ireland while the Trailers people were prominent businessmen. Even at this early stage, however, there were tensions between the various groups and these preparatory meetings were chaired alternately by James MacQuitty and George MacKean. For me the objectives were clear: time was already perilously short and we had just one month to find enough backing from suitable investors. After an exchange of views we were sent forth with urgent instructions to persuade friends and associates to risk their money on this apparently dubious enterprise – a task made much more difficult because our rivals in the Abercorn group had a head start and were generally viewed as odds-on favourites.

Bill was an enthusiastic fundraiser while I, as a young though vigorous and committed player in this game, was mainly a middleman between the various groups: the Trailers people, the London people, the aristocrats and the Hendersons. Keeping everybody on board was no easy matter and there were problems from the outset. One was the constitution of the Board. After difficult negotiations it was agreed that all four factions would be represented in strictly defined proportions. My father and brother were to be the Henderson Board members (partly because I was the youngest but also because I might act as a bridge to Uncle James who was not told about our involvement yet). Another delicate question was who should be chairman.

George MacKean was offered the post and declined it, proposing instead the Earl of Antrim, and though there were some who favoured Lord O'Neill and others who wanted one of the MacQuittys it was Lord Antrim who eventually carried the day. We also needed to give the Board some civil service gravitas – someone who knew the Whitehall ropes and might pull the odd string for us. In this role we cast (and I recruited) the admirable and elegant Sir Francis Evans, an Ulsterman who had been Ambassador to Israel and Consul General in New York. Another who joined the Board was Marcia Mackie, vice-chairman of the Northern Ireland Hospitals Authority but a suggestion that we recruit the carpet millionaire Cyril Lord was rejected (one member observing tartly that 'we are over-Lorded already').

We sought at the same time to include investors from across Northern Ireland and on that basis brought on to the Board Patrick Herdman, the chairman of his family firm in Strabane. Meanwhile, drawing on my News Letter background, I canvassed owners or editors of some of the county weekly newspapers such as Bertie Trimble of the *Impartial Reporter* in Enniskillen, Stanley Wilson of the *Tyrone Constitution* and Jim Morton and Courtney Hutchinson of the *Lurgan Mail*. All of them invested, forming a group with one seat on the Board.

The allocation of shares caused much wrangling, some of it very unpleasant. On the one hand there were those who openly wanted the biggest stake they could get, an approach which prompted jealousy and suspicion elsewhere, while on the other almost everybody occasionally had cold feet about the whole enterprise. Levels of anxiety were kept high by a steady flow of opinions – usually wildly conflicting – from advertising luminaries such as Dan Ingman of Young and Rubicam, about the prospects for the local market. A bad forecast would send investors into a flutter while a good one would intensify the arguments about shares. One investor we lost along the way was Lord Dunleath, who decided his family trustees would not permit such a hazardous investment (much later, as we shall see in another chapter, his views were to change).

On to all these troubled waters I poured what oil I could but ultimately it was between the heavyweights that matters were settled. The London group of William MacQuitty, Sir Laurence Olivier and Betty Box each took 8 per cent of the £100,000 capital of the company, giving them a combined holding of just under one quarter. This was fair, not least because as things transpired they were more ready than most to come up with their money in full and on time. The local investors took up at this stage a total of 51 per cent, with the maximum stake for any individual set at £2,500. We Hendersons – my father, Bill and I – each put up £1,700, giving us a shade over 5 per cent. Like everybody else we were liable for double the sum invested if things went wrong, so we were acutely conscious that, as with those Associated-Rediffusion men, we were taking a risk that could cost us dear. Finally there remained 25 per cent of stock unissued; this was to be allocated if and when we won the contract, with members of the losing consortium among the targets.

An important issue relating to the composition of the group was tackled soon after my arrival. Along with one or two other members I had noticed that both our consortium and the Duke of Abercorn's had a significant omission – no Catholics. Looking back from this distance in time it may seem incredible that this was not a priority from the outset but it is a measure of how different Northern Ireland was then that it was not. Our group, however, had received a tip that the Authority (which as it happens was then chaired by a Catholic, Sir Ivone Kirkpatrick) considered it important that the winner of the Northern Ireland contract should have an 'across the board' character. When this intelligence reached us quite a few refused to take it seriously: the project was a massive gamble anyway, they said, so why complicate it with religion and politics? Happily those views did not carry the day. We already had one Catholic shareholder in our midst, albeit an English one, in Lady Antrim, and we set about recruiting more. The educationalist J.J. Campbell took a stake, as did the Belfast businessman Frank Benner, Cyril Nicholson Q.C. and two Ballymena solicitors, the brothers Francis and John McCann. Taken together they were still a small proportion of our investors, but the Board decided that if we won the contract our unissued shares would be offered as a priority to further potential Catholic investors. This commitment was written into our bid document.

If this inclusiveness, which was to prove extremely important, appears opportunistic I should say that it was not. In my own short career, and in my father's longer one, it had always been an abiding principle that the minority community should so far as possible be drawn in to the life of Northern Ireland. I remember well my father's bitter regret in Government House days when invitations to the Catholic clergy were not accepted. I too had argued frequently in the columns of the *News Letter* against Nationalist abstentionism at Stormont, urging the Nationalist leaders to take up the opportunities for criticism which were open to them, on the grounds that rejection only served to make the lot of Catholics more difficult. More than that, as I have shown in the preceding chapters, my education and personal attitudes had led me to a relatively apolitical view of Northern Ireland and though I supported the Union I was much less 'Orange' than many people assumed. I disliked the parochialism and narrowness of much of Ulster life and believed that the future for everyone lay in greater tolerance and a willingness to look forward and outward. Some of us in the consortium, moreover, felt it was essential for a commercial television station to command all round loyalty and to be fair and even-handed – 'middle-of-the-road', if you like.

Besides the personalities, the finance and the politics, there was also the overarching matter of producing a document to impress and delight the ITA, and this was what Paddy Falloon had in mind when he spoke to me of needing 'someone to do some writing'. For three desperate weeks leading up to the October deadline a drafting committee laboured night after night into the small hours and I was at the heart of this effort. The other committee members were a lively bunch. Hubert Wilmot, the founder of the Belfast Arts Theatre, was a dynamic and creative man who had been brought in at my suggestion – indeed he had attended that first meeting at the Trailers offices. Robert Frizzell, general manager of the Northern Ireland Tourist Board, was another useful contact of mine; it was through his good offices that I had been able to bring Sir Francis Evans on to the Board. Also on the drafting committee were Anthony Lucy, a Belfast architect, and of course my brother Bill. Sydney Box lent a hand, too; I remember him rolling up his sleeves for one Sunday morning session in the Crawfordsburn Inn and making a tremendous contribution. In this work, it should be said, we were largely uninhibited by knowledge, for not a single member of the group had any experience of, or familiarity with, television. Thus, while BBC Northern Ireland was content at that time to produce a mere five minutes' television a day in the form of a single news bulletin read by a single announcer, we were free to promise a glittering range of home-grown programmes. I blush now to think of what we suggested and it is certain that if we had tried to implement them all straight away we would have been bankrupt in weeks. But this was an application and as with most applications we gilded the lily in every way short of perjury, and not only in the field of programmes. Every Board member and significant investor, for example, had to be announced with all possible grandiloquence, as if he or she were a person of such outstanding merit and importance that their mere involvement was proof we would succeed. This trick presented no difficulty in the case of the great Olivier but with others more effort was needed. When for example I asked the unassuming Pat Herdman to list his qualifications he wrote simply 'M.F.H.'. Once I had worked out that this meant Master of Fox Hounds I reflected (wrongly, perhaps) that it would not impress metropolitan ITA bureaucrats and so I wrote instead about his many public services and charitable activities. We also promised to have advisory committees on every kind of worthy subject, each of them peopled by the most illustrious do-gooders in their fields – some of whom were never consulted about their inclusion, and at least one of whom was dead at the time.

That we were not even more reckless we probably owed to the urbane and soft-spoken Sydney. He at least had the experience of having been involved in the successful bid for Tyne Tees Television and on his advice some of our wilder flights of fancy were tempered. Thus the confident 'will' was replaced by a conditional 'may', 'plans' became 'aspirations' and 'aims' became 'philosophies'. Sydney also contributed memorably to the general well-being when, after a particularly brain-numbing session, he introduced me to the pleasures of the Negroni, a cocktail of gin, Campari, Italian vermouth and soda – lethal but lovely.

In the panicky final days, with some of us burning candles at both ends, the document was knocked into shape. Names had been chosen, numbers (however speculative) added up and fine words fell into place. Just before the deadline I packed Joy, Glynis, baby Sally and the precious draft into the company Ford and drove to London. Depositing the family in Chiswick with our old Trinity friends Nan and Glyn Owen, I headed out on the Sunday morning to Mill Hill for a final session with Sydney Box and William MacQuitty. The amended version I then posted back to Bill at the *News Letter*, where he had it printed and bound in an elegant light blue cover. This completed document was despatched post-haste back to London, reaching the ITA with hours to spare on 9th October. So hurried was the procedure that the final version was seen by only a minority of the proposed Board members listed in its sonorous opening pages and by almost none of the 'ordinary' investors. Four weeks later the interviews were conducted and our team, comprising Lord Antrim, William MacQuitty, my brother Bill and our wise and persuasive family accountant, George Cameron, flew over to be grilled by the Authority. They found themselves sharing the plane with the Duke of Abercorn and his team and were even more surprised to see that the Cunninghams had shotguns in their luggage – relaxed and confident, they intended to make a weekend of it on the grouse moors. To the very last, word of mouth in Northern Ireland and in the television industry still suggested that the Abercorn group would defeat us.

They did not. On Guy Fawkes Day, 1958, the day after the interviews, the ITA announced that it had chosen our group. It would be nice to say that I remember celebrations – if such a thing happened today the champagne would certainly flow - but there were none. The times were more straight-laced; the members of the consortium were hard-headed and not especially friendly with one another; the investors were also chillingly aware that this decision meant their money was now on the line. I do remember a mood of great surprise because everyone, not least ourselves, was astonished that we had pulled it off. For years afterwards James MacQuitty used to recall the dry remark of a colleague at the Bar who on hearing the news exclaimed: 'James, dear boy, democracy has at long last come to Northern Ireland…' He waited for James to pull a baffled face before completing his line: '…when an Earl can defeat a Duke.' Why the Earl of Antrim's bid had been chosen ahead of the Duke of Abercorn's was not immediately clear but is now a matter of record, for the official history of ITV records of our group: 'Its statement of intent seemed fuller and its membership seemed more widely representative of Northern Ireland as a whole.' This was a clear vindication of our policy of inclusiveness, of drawing in investors both from across Northern Ireland - Pat Herdman and the weekly papers, for example - and from the Catholic community.

So far as I was concerned, this was where my involvement ended. The capture of the contract, I thought, marked the end of my short professional involvement with television. I was not even on the Board of the new company so all that remained for me was to return to my job at the *News Letter* and hope that my investment would bring a good return. In fact there was quite a bit of tidying up to be done and I played my part. We offered shares to the defeated parties, of whom the Duke accepted and the *Northern Whig* declined, and to a variety of others. The *Irish News* took a stake - Ann McCollum, a member of the Fitzpatrick family who owned the paper, later joined the Board. Two other Catholics who invested and also became Board members were Mon O'Driscoll, a local stockbroker, and Brian McGuckian, a figure of international standing in the pig trade. Contrary to all expectation, another who was persuaded to buy shares was Uncle James. From day one all three of us had dreaded the moment when he would learn of our role in the bid but we underestimated him, for the anticipated explosion never came. Mostly through my father's efforts he was induced to put up £2,500 of the paper's cash for a further stake to underpin the Henderson presence in the new company although he made it plain that he thought it was a case of throwing good money after bad. 'Your father and brother are mad,' he announced to me. Meantime I was doing my best to smooth the way for the new arrival in the local 'media', and again this was not easy. Despite Uncle James's change of heart on the money the *News Letter* remained unenthusiastic while over at the *Belfast Telegraph* the editor, Jack Sayers, actually declared war on the commercial station on the grounds that it was a rival not only for advertising but also for editorial influence. After doing what I could in these small matters I returned with a mixture of relief and regret to my old, less hectic life.

Weeks passed and then one day in January 1959 I bumped into Lord Antrim in Donegall Street. I asked cheerfully how things were going and to my shock he replied with feeling that they were 'bloody awful'. A rift had opened between himself, as chairman, and William MacQuitty, the film producer who was now managing director, and it seemed that progress towards getting the station on air was proving painfully slow. Amazed, I asked a few basic questions about where things stood, to which he confessed that he did not know the answers. He asked me to put them in writing along with any other thoughts I had and said he would pass them to Howard Thomas. Thomas was the managing director of ABC, the big ITV company then broadcasting at weekends in the Midlands and north of England, and I knew that ABC had been appointed to advise the fledgling Northern Ireland station. (In retrospect it was a measure of how bad things were that the company chairman should have found himself relying on an outsider such as Thomas, and indeed on me, in quite this way.) I duly sat down and wrote out a list of some forty questions on what I thought were the relevant matters – programme plans, recruitment, equipment, premises, public relations, advertising sales and so forth. A fortnight later Lord Antrim called me back to say that Thomas was unable to answer all of my questions but had suggested that whoever asked them should be brought in to run the company. Flattering as this was I could not take it seriously and pointed out that it was much easier to ask questions than to answer them. But the matter did not rest there.

A week later I received an invitation to dinner with two of Howard's senior executives, Michael Hutcheson and Tom Singleton, who were now also involved in helping the new station. It was a pleasant occasion. These were showbiz people of the kind I had come to like in my Dublin Players days and we talked generally about their early experiences in ITV and about the prospects for the new company. These prospects, I knew, were looking brighter in one important respect, for ABC's powerful advertising director, George Cooper, had recently paid a visit to Belfast and pronounced that there was every potential for a healthy market. But it was also clear that the Board of the new company, which had been troubled from the outset, was now woefully divided. The two ABC men urged me to come in and run the operation but again I hesitated; I was worried about what lay behind those boardroom divisions and I was also uncertain about myself. I was only 29 years old, after all, with a wife and family to support, and I knew next to nothing about broadcasting. Would the thing last? Would I be up to the job? Or would I merely be mincemeat between those factions on the Board? I kept my distance.

Another week passed and another agreeable dinner took place, this time accompanied by a firm offer of a position in executive control of the company, with clear terms and a personal guarantee from Lord Antrim. Yes, they said, I had much to learn about television but that need not be a problem; I already knew a fair amount about news, advertising, theatre and films and these were after all at the heart of the medium. I also had a lot of friends, and Northern Ireland is a small place where friendships count. Daunted though I was, by now I was becoming aware that this was something I wanted, a chance to marry my showbiz instincts with my newspaper and business background, a golden opportunity for a new career entirely of my own. In fact the more I had thought about it the more I was sure that for me it was the job of a lifetime. I could not turn it down again and, although it took them yet another long lunch to convince me entirely, in the end I said I would do it. What was I to be called? 'Managing Director' was already taken, although William MacQuitty only held the post part-time. Other companies had a 'Station Controller' or a 'Chief Executive', but I became 'General Manager'. Another and more uncomfortable formality was that ITA rules required the senior hired hand (which I would become) to be on the Board and this meant that because of the delicate balance of Board membership either my brother or my father would soon have to step down. Lord Antrim spoke discreetly to my father, who resigned to make way for me, a characteristically generous and honourable decision, though one that was made with a heavy heart. He had been the first to suggest a commercial station in Northern Ireland and he had been eager to play a part in making it work. Fortunately I knew nothing of this until it was over.

The same could not be said about my resignation from the *News Letter*, which naturally had to be presented in person to Uncle James. 'It's a pity,' he declared, on hearing that I was to desert the ancient family firm for a despised new medium. 'I was going to leave you my shares...' He sighed and then observed somewhat sourly: 'I suppose they are paying you plenty in that television thing.' I explained that I would earn twice what I had at the *News Letter* and he just grunted. We parted, nevertheless, amiably enough and in the event he did not disinherit me. With characteristic stubbornness, however, he held me to every single day of my notice period, so that although I accepted the job in March and was desperate to start, it was not until 1st May 1959 – still three months short of my 30th birthday – that I was able formally to take up my post at Ulster Television.

5
Hallowe'en Launch

Our ambitious target for the start of broadcasting was 31st October 1959 – Hallowe'en – so on the May Day morning when I first sat in the General Manager's chair exactly six months remained in which to create a television station. To say that the beginnings were small would be over-generous, for the full-time staff comprised just three people: myself, my old Brackenber friend Barry Johnston, who was already on board to run the finances, and another Johnston, Valerie, who had been found by Lord Antrim and who became my first secretary. Our offices at 43 Donegall Street, a few yards from the *News Letter*, were owned by one of our bigger shareholders, Ivan Pollin. They were small and rudimentary, although Valerie was exaggerating when she observed to a *Daily Mail* journalist that she was 'sitting in a garret with a drip on the end of my nose' (a remark which duly appeared in print and did not impress Ivan).

The finding of proper premises to accommodate all the various facets of a television company was an urgent priority and the quest ranged over no fewer than 57 possible sites around Belfast. I favoured a location by the River Lagan opposite Stranmillis College but the Board deemed this too expensive and instead they bought a derelict former hemstitching factory and warehouse on the Ormeau Road, costing £17,000. William MacQuitty romantically dubbed it a 'little gem' but visitors over the years have been surprised both by the workmanlike Victorian exterior and the location – not in Belfast's business centre or some leafy suburb but opposite the gasworks on the edge of a district of redbrick terraces. The Board was later to promise a move to custom-built premises by the Lagan, but the promise was never kept. Havelock House, therefore, became and remained our home.

The next important job was recruitment. We needed a staff of around 80 by air date and our advertisements produced no fewer than 8,000 responses. The application form we then prepared caused the first dispute between Barry Johnston and myself for a line at the end asked applicants to 'state religion'. Although this was standard practice in Northern Ireland it seemed to me inappropriate and likely to foster the impression of discrimination, something which I felt the company must avoid. I explained this to Barry and said the forms could not be used. He saw my point but as our chief (and only) accountant he felt he had to insist. 'It's too late,' he said. 'This will cost too much money.' He also had a point – there were 8,000 of these documents and printing was not cheap – but I refused to budge. After some tense exchanges an idea came to me that broke the deadlock. I took the boxes round to the *News Letter* printing department and asked the man who operated the paper guillotine to chop off the offending part of each form. He did a neat job, the forms were despatched and an old friendship was saved. In the end we interviewed some 800 people, a prodigious and exhausting task.

The ball was now rolling and we had plenty of work on our hands but I was aware that the biggest problem of all had yet to be tackled. This was the tension and nervousness within the Board. The issue, inevitably, was money, for after winning the contract the main investors – all represented on the Board – received a rude shock. It had been known from the outset that the company would have to pay an annual rental to the ITA of more than £100,000, a huge sum equivalent to half our total capitalisation. It had become clear also that our bid had seriously underestimated other costs, both in terms of capital spending in Belfast and of various services we would need to pay for when we were broadcasting. The prospect of profit appeared to be receding into a dim and uncertain future while the possibility of crippling losses seemed ever more real. In this climate every penny spent on the embryonic station looked to many Board members like money down the drain and the inevitable result was paralysis. We needed hard decisions.

The key was a sharp revision of our production ideas. Home grown programmes were far more expensive than ones bought off the network or from elsewhere so that was the natural place for economies. Those grandiose 'aspirations' in our contract application, assembled with such enthusiasm the previous autumn, had come to appear not just over-ambitious but foolhardy, and the necessary revision was painful. One sad casualty was Hubert 'Hibbie' Wilmot, who had laboured so hard on the bid and was earmarked for the post of Programme Controller. He had been despatched to other ITV companies to learn the ropes and had achieved an impressive technical mastery to go with his creative gift, but he fell foul of William MacQuitty and some of the other 'hard-headed' members of the Board. His flair and liveliness, which had seemed such an asset, now appeared to them to be a threat to their investment. I protested but lacked the clout to change their minds, and so in a sorry scene – 'Of course you will still be a producer for us, darling' – William put paid to Hibbie's television ambitions.

Even when we had scrapped plans for various weekly programmes the economies were insufficient and I knew the axe must fall next on news. We had promised regular local bulletins but it was clear that even the most modest news service would be disproportionately expensive both in hardware and staff. I therefore recommended that, while we would carry national and international news via the network from ITN, we should offer no local service. Viewers who wanted to hear about events in Ulster would have to switch over to BBC to watch their short bulletins. For me this was a matter of regret – I was a journalist, I loved news and I thought this was an area where we could really do something – but we had to cut our suit according to our cloth, and with the Board so nervous we had very little of that. I was still convinced that the company would succeed and make money and that this was a postponement rather than a cancellation.

Once the new plan was in place, however, a stark fact was evident: so much had been thrown out that apart from a few 'specials' sprinkled over the early months of broadcasting it looked as though local programmes would be limited to one single daily show. I put all our eggs in one basket and that basket was *Roundabout*. This was a happy idea – good enough, we thought, to convince our viewers, our advertisers and our own staff (once we had one) that we really meant business. The origin of the show lay in the idea that even if we could not have news we could still make a contribution in current affairs. So we planned a programme which brought Ulster life in its many forms into our one small studio each night. The brief was wide, embracing the arts, business, agriculture, sport and matters of small-scale local interest as well as politics and general events, and the tone would be as relaxed and accessible as current television conventions allowed. Essentially a complement to the Belfast newspapers (which we shamelessly plundered for ideas), *Roundabout* was to run for half an hour in a teatime slot every weekday. Seen from a distance of more than 40 years this formula appears all too familiar – today such shows fill a large slice of the daytime schedule – but in 1959 it was ground-breaking; in fact it was the first nightly magazine programme on British regional television. We had high hopes of it.

All of this re-planning did not escape the notice of the ITA, whose job it was to protect the public interest and ensure that the stations fulfilled their contracts. Sir Robert Fraser, the director-general, was keeping a close eye on developments and we were still months from the air date with our plans far from finalized when William MacQuitty and I were summoned to his offices in Princes Gate, Kensington, to give an account of ourselves. This first formal encounter with Fraser began with a curious little scene. Just after we had taken our seats there came a slight buzzing from somewhere inside the DG's desk. With some irritation he strode across, opened a drawer and pulled out a telephone receiver, declaring firmly: 'I said I was not to be disturbed.' There was a little pause, and then 'Tell Downing Street I am in an important meeting and not available,' after which the receiver was replaced and the drawer slid shut. I suppose it could have been anybody in Downing Street calling but our vanity was tickled. The cosy feeling did not last long for Sir Robert went on to give us a thorough grilling about our plans.

Lord Antrim had laid some groundwork in a letter setting out the financial difficulties and pointing out in particular that our annual rental payment to the ITA now looked not only crippling but also unfair. This payment had been calculated in accordance with a population formula applied elsewhere in ITV but we believed this was wrong because a far smaller proportion of people had televisions in Northern Ireland than, say, in the south of England. We would be paying our rental, therefore, on the basis of the total population but selling advertising - and thus earning income - on the basis of a much lower number of people with televisions. We thought it was a good argument but Sir Robert would not budge. His position was that we had known when we applied for the contract what the rental would be and whatever we now thought about the formula we were stuck with it. No amount of argument or pleading, no dire warnings that the station might go under, made any difference. Elsewhere, though, he was more flexible, even helpful. I suspect that the ITA had known all along that our original bid was too ambitious and was prepared to see the programme plans severely curtailed at launch so, although we were made to sweat our scaled-down plans eventually won approval. Most difficult was the dropping of the news service, which ran pretty close to the ITA's public service brief. Sir Robert was very unhappy with this, and took me to task personally as a former journalist but slowly warmed to the idea that *Roundabout*, which I sold to him as a local version of the BBC's highly-regarded *Tonight* programme, might be a sort of substitute. It would cover local affairs, I insisted, and carry serious interviews, as well as giving a local feel to the whole UTV output. A little grudgingly he gave it his blessing on the condition that we undertook to handle real, hard news in *Roundabout* if big stories broke. He emphasized that this dispensation was temporary and that he expected a gradual increase in our output and, in particular, the introduction of a news service as soon as income permitted. Naturally we agreed.

We were by now finding our screen talent. Of those 800 people we interviewed for jobs in all parts of the company, about 80 had been judged to have potential as presenters. Just six positions were available so the number was whittled down until we had the team we wanted. Two of the most important posts were those presenting *Roundabout,* and they went to interesting characters. One was Ivor Mills, then in his early twenties and a music teacher. He had a certain sharpness of feature and of mind and also great resources of instinct, and he was to prove a charming interviewer who could be tough when necessary. The other was Anne Gregg, a 19-year-old whose amateur acting experience stood her in good stead. Our first announcers, who would link the programmes, were both theatre professionals: Adrienne McGuill, who subsequently earned a place in Ulster folklore as 'Miss Adrienne', and Jimmy Greene, whom I had seen performing at Hubert Wilmot's Arts Theatre. Jimmy later succeeded Ivor Mills on *Roundabout* before returning to the stage. Fifth of the six was another announcer, Brian Durkin, a Newry teacher with a degree from Queen's who had experience in drama, in his case as an amateur. His appeal was more rugged, and he would later go on to work in Yorkshire and then Scottish Television. Last but not least came our sports presenter. Although our slender resources would prevent us showing much sport we were keen to provide a decent preview of the weekend's events in the Friday night edition of *Roundabout,* discussing imminent fixtures and giving an idea of the prospects. For this role we chose an old friend of mine, Ernest Strathdee, a former rugby star who played in the great Irish Triple Crown side of 1948. (He was the scrum half whose job was to feed the ball to the great Jack Kyle.) Since then Ernie had come close to entering the Presbyterian ministry but he was delighted by his break into showbusiness and made such a good job of it that he soon extended his role beyond sport.

I must mention one other talented person who came to my notice at this time. Through the old pals' network I was persuaded to interview a Portadown girl of just 16 who, though still at school, was apparently desperate for a job on the small screen. I soon saw that she had great potential for she was a delightful young woman in character as well as appearance. She had been studying music, was

A formal portrait of my father, Commander Oscar Henderson (Comptroller in the Governor of Northern Ireland's household), in full regalia, and my mother, Molly, in her elegant gown for presentation at Court

A family group photograph taken on the garden steps at Government House, Hillsborough. Left to right: my brother Bill, Dad, me, Mum and Nurse Warnock

Members of the royal family regularly visited Government House. This photograph (taken at Clandeboye) marked the visit of the Duke and Duchess of York to Ulster in 1924 – the Duchess (later Queen Elizabeth, the Queen Mother) was a favourite visitor.

The teens – at last

A production of *Hamlet* at Bradfield College, 1946. Plays in Greek were produced biennially at Bradfield but during the Second World War we resorted to Shakespeare – a shade more comprehensible.

Trinity College Historical Society (the 'Hist') Committee, 1950. I am fourth from the left in the back row, with Henry Clark (later M.P.) on my right.

The 1960s Ulster Television Board. From bottom left: Paddy Falloon (hotelier and industrialist); Marcia Mackie (Chair of the Northern Ireland Hospital Authority); Brian McGuckian (international pig breeder); Courtney Catherwood (building industrialist); Lady Antrim (sculptress); behind, far left, Barry Johnston (Company Secretary); on his right, Professor James Montrose; William MacQuitty; Lord Antrim; me; to my left, Michael Hutcheson (Sales Director); Captain Bill Henderson; James MacQuitty Q.C.; Stanley Wilson (*Tyrone Constitution*); Mon O'Driscoll (stockbroker); Major George Mackean

Sir Laurence Olivier giving Ulster Television's opening night epilogue – Addison's 'The Spacious Firmament', 31st October 1959

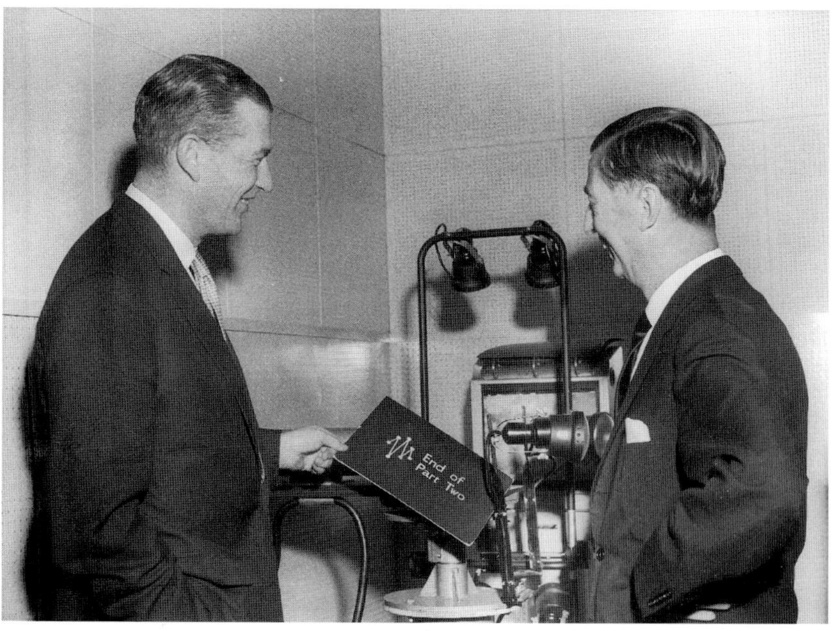

With the great Sir Robert Fraser – first Director General of the ITA (c.1960)

Our first news magazine programme, *Roundabout*, put UTV in touch with the people and the people in touch with us. Here, presenter Ivor Mills shares a joke with Norman Vaughn

Tommy James – our 'Mr Music' – charms Lord Aylestone as he did our audience nightly

With Bruce Forsyth in the 1960s

Outside Havelock House with Captain Terence O'Neill on his accession as Prime Minister of Northern Ireland

With Lord Erskine of Rerrick (penultimate Governor of Northern Ireland) in the 1960s

With Bill (Sir William) Brown of Scottish Television when we retrieved the Natural Break trophy after some years of defeat in the 1960s

In the studio, in the 70s

The Standing Consultative Committee of ITV, 1970 – the chief executives of the 15 independent television stations. Standing, left to right: Anthony Gorard (Harlech); Aubrey Buxton (Anglia); David Wilson (Southern); me; Alex Mair (Grampian); James Bredin (Border); Kenneth Killip (Channel); Tom Margerison (LWT); Bernard Sendall (ITA); Anthony Jelly (Tyne-Tees); Anthony Pragnell (ITA). Seated, left to right: Denis Forman (Granada); G.E. Ward Thomas (Yorkshire); Howard Thomas (Thames); Sir Robert Fraser; Lord Aylestone (ITA); Cecil Bernstein (Granada); Lew Grade (ATV); the Earl of Lisburne (Westward TV)

With Lord Grey, the last Governor of Northern Ireland

With the American evangelist Dr Billy Graham in the early 1970s

Gordon Burns (left) and Joan Trimble of the *Impartial Reporter* – and a distinguished musician – with myself and Ian Sanderson (News Editor), c.1970. Joan was being inducted to our board.

Robin Harris chairs a heated General Election post-mortem discussion between the Rev Ian Paisley (Democratic Unionist), Robin Chichester-Clark (Ulster Unionist) and David Bleakley (N.I. Labour Party); Gordon Burns looks on.

One of television's best-loved talents, Gloria Hunniford, here pictured with Hughie Green

Irish traditional music was another pioneering UTV programme venture in the 1970s (its progenitor, Brian O'Donnell, at curtain)

The Troubles took their toll on Havelock House – here we are guarded after the fire-bomb attack of 1977

Pat with Jane and Humphrey ('Who?') Atkins on his arrival to Northern Ireland as Secretary of State, 1979

Lord Antrim's quizzical stare on Betty MacQuitty (with Bill extreme right) and Sir Francis Evans (deeply attentive), 1970s accustomed to public performance of various kinds and clearly had the necessary spark to engage the viewer. For all her promise, though, she was too young and inexperienced and so, not quite repeating Noel Coward's advice to Mrs Worthington, I told her to go back to school, finish her exams and then see if she could get a job on a local paper or in a dance or music school; after that if we had a vacancy we would get in touch. This wise advice was comprehensively ignored; a few months later I was walking past our advertising sales office and spotted that same blonde head bent over the outgoing mail, sorting letters and licking stamps. Gloria Hunniford was not to be put off her career in broadcasting as easily as that.

Behind the scenes we still had the support and advice of the ABC people and we recruited a dozen of their technical and production staff from Manchester, some of them with Irish links. One of these was Frank Brady, whom we chose as our Chief Engineer. Frank was a Catholic from Navan in the Irish Republic and his provenance ruffled some feathers. At that time anyone from outside the United Kingdom taking up such a post needed a work permit and these were issued only in circumstances where suitable native labour was not available. There was a delay with the issuing of Frank's permit and eventually I was sent for personally by the Minister for Labour at Stormont, Major Ivan Neill, to account for the choice. (I subsequently learned to my dismay that this move was prompted by a member of my own Board.) Neill, to his credit, was clearly embarrassed and unhesitatingly accepted my assurance that people with experience in television engineering were in such short supply that local preference was simply not possible. The permit was duly issued. Another man who came to us from ABC was (Colonel) S.E. Reynolds, who took the post of Programme Controller left open by the departure of Hibbie Wilmot. He was 63 and had been around a bit, having run a circus at one stage and then become one of the first ever television producers, making *Picture Box* for the BBC at Alexandra Palace before the war. I liked him instantly when we first met in June 1959 and looked forward to heaping a lot of work on to his shoulders but, just as the appointment was made, he revealed he was about to have an operation and would be out of action until five weeks before our air date. ABC's 'favour' was thus a mixed blessing, in the short term at least.

While the staff was taking shape I also had other tasks. First, we needed an audience, and nothing illustrates more vividly than this how different life was then, for in the Northern Ireland of 1959 the new medium was very new indeed. The very first local broadcasts, only in the Belfast area, had been of the Queen's coronation in 1953 – a mere six years earlier. I remembered this well because I had written about the occasion in the *News Letter*. It was not until 1955 that the Divis transmitter made the BBC signal available in theory to two-thirds of the population, but this was a privilege which not every household had chosen to exercise or could afford to exercise. There were fewer than 50,000 households in Northern Ireland with televisions and most of those had sets which could only receive one channel. We needed to improve on this dramatically and for this job I asked the Board for £10,000. Although some members were so shocked that they began to wonder aloud whether my appointment might have been a mistake, I got the money, appointed an advertising agency, McConnell's, to promote us in the local press, in shops and through posters, and recruited a *Belfast Telegraph* journalist, Gordon Duffield, as our full-time PR man. The message was simple: the new channel would not only double the available programming but would also offer more 'popular' style and content. As I saw it, and as I told all our staff when they joined us, our aim was television for the Shankill and Falls Roads rather than for the Malone and Antrim Roads which, in my view, had the BBC to cater to them. Over the months, by every means we could think of, we drove home that message far and wide. By now we had a logo as well as a name to give us an identity, having staged a competition to discover something that would be striking but uncontroversial. The result, which survived for 40 years was the zig-zag line, up and down from left to right. Many tried to imbue it with some deep meaning – did the six segments, for example, refer to the six counties? – but it was in fact no more than an artistic representation of an electronic scanning dot.

Meanwhile our transmitter, or rather the ITA transmitter which would carry our signal, was slowly rising over Black Mountain to the west of Belfast, a very visible symbol of our presence. Indeed it was so visible it acquired among my friends the nickname of 'Brum's thing'. Soon it was putting out a test card on channel nine, accompanied by a message spoken by the actor Maurice O'Callaghan – with a second one, for the sake of variety, in my own voice – urging people to 'Prepare in time for Channel Nine'. This happy slogan was all my own work and was only later rivalled for wit and imagination by my follow-up to promote our Strabane booster signal: 'Don't be late for Channel Eight'. All these promotional efforts had their effect, in spreading the word, establishing our identity and above all encouraging a sizeable jump in the sales of television sets. Given the suspicion persisting in some parts of the Northern Ireland press and the hostility of the local BBC – I remember having some sparky public debates with the BBC Controller, Robert McCall – the Board's money was very well spent.

Advertising of the other sort – the kind that would bring in revenue – was another area where we were indebted to ABC, in many ways godfather to Ulster Television. They sold 'time' for us nationally on a percentage basis, with Michael Hutcheson in charge, as it was considered too expensive to establish our own sales force in London. The rapid rise in television sales helped Mike, as did the somewhat surprised discovery by people in the business that Northern Ireland folk actually needed and sometimes even used the detergents and toothpastes that were then the mainstay of ITV advertising. We also began selling local advertising on our own behalf in Northern Ireland, with Basil Lapworth, a former salesman at Rank and a former manager of the Hippodrome, in charge. Probably our most attractive offer was the simple slide promotion, a humble still picture with text and voiceover, and though these were crude by modern standards they gave the output a homely flavour. It would make a big difference to our appeal if Ulster Television was not only promoting Surf and Pepsodent, but also car dealerships on the Newtownards Road and animal feed producers in Cookstown. And the slides were very good value at a mere £1 per second on the screen when a quarter of a million potential customers might be watching.

Those six months from May to October were hard but, when Hallowe'en arrived, we were ready. We had our home, our staff, our equipment, our advertisements, our schedule and our place in the airwaves; all that remained was to please the audience. The final stage of preparation was the publication, on the preceding Thursday, of the first edition of our own listings paper, a slim tabloid on ordinary newsprint called *TV Post*. Produced out of our original little office in Donegall Street, this was a lively offering carrying details of the week's output plus, in that original issue, a glowing introduction to the company. *TV Post* was to become a great asset.

The night before the launch was bizarre. I formed part of the reception committee at Nutts Corner, then Belfast's airport, when our VIP guests arrived for the occasion. No sooner had the plane landed than the airport lights failed and in the torchlit blundering which followed the comedienne Beatrice Lillie (in real life Lady Peel and a native of Hillsborough, Co. Down), one of our honoured guests, missed her footing on the aircraft steps and was plunging towards the tarmac when I managed to catch her in my arms. Then Sir Laurence Olivier, carrying his own luggage, found himself rebuffed from all the bigger limousines, which had been reserved for ITA grandees, and ended up in my modest Humber Hawk. He was curiously quiet on the journey to his hotel in town, and more so when the receptionist there failed to recognize him, made him spell his name for her and stubbornly addressed him as 'Mr Oliver'.

As for the launch day itself, we had given ourselves plenty of time for rehearsal so a certain amount of precision was evident, but we were naturally worried that a bungle might reduce us to a laughing-stock or worse. I dealt with this in the only way I knew, probably learned in my college days on the stage: I told myself not to feel anything at all, just to maintain a steely resolve, to smile and be courteous and keep things rolling no matter what. The proceedings began with a solemn lunch given by the ITA at the Grand Central Hotel, an occasion enlivened by the interjections of Bea Lillie. This sparky lady, one of our smaller shareholders and my neighbour at the table, was determined to have some fun and our noisy conversation attracted some disapproving looks. Lunch over, we adjourned to Havelock House and, at 4.45 p.m., our 405-line black-and-white signal went on air with a short word from Olivier, introducing Lord Wakehurst, the Governor of Northern Ireland, who solemnly welcomed us into the world. Then came a live, locally-produced children's show in which a collection of youngsters plucked from nearby streets ducked for apples and engaged in other Hallowe'en pursuits. Beatrice Lillie acted as hostess and she carried it off with great style and charm, chatting merrily to the children and the viewers. This was followed by a short tour of Northern Ireland in words and music and a series of recorded greetings from ITV stars, and after that we launched into the first episode of *The Adventures of Robin Hood* starring Richard Greene. Bea Lillie, meanwhile, adjourned to the boardroom, where to the bemusement of assembled worthies such as Lord Wakehurst and Lord Brookeborough, the Prime Minister, she produced a shambling, tweed-coated man and formally introduced him. 'May I present my agent, Philip Huck?' she said, adding with relish: 'You spell it with an H.' This was not in our script.

On the screen, after *Robin Hood*, the evening steadily unfolded with the ITN news, *77 Sunset Strip*, a Jimmy Jewel variety programme from London, wrestling and a Gary Cooper movie. This was network stuff, a lot less high-risk than the live studio programme at the start, but still I could not relax and so as I smiled confidently and steered Bea Lillie towards safer waters, a procession of possible disasters was running continuously through my mind. Then I found an unexpected cause for concern: Olivier.

Ever since he became involved with Ulster Television as a shareholder I had nursed hopes of using his talents as well as his money and I was delighted when he agreed to be the first face to appear on air. That was a matter of a very few words, but we had also persuaded him to do a reading of some sort at the end of the evening's broadcast. There had been no opportunity to rehearse this and we had not even established what he wanted to read. On the day, therefore, when the opportunity arose, I asked him: something appropriate from the Bible, perhaps, or a little Shakespeare...? He chose instead Addison's poem 'The Spacious Firmament'. I knew instantly that we had no copy of it and since by then the shops were on the point of closing, someone was despatched in all haste to find, at any price, the most luxurious edition Belfast could offer. Once it arrived, and while *Robin Hood*, Jimmy Jewel *et al.* were on air, we conducted a couple of belated rehearsals which, largely because our staff were nervous in the company of this great man, were clumsy and embarrassing. As the vision loomed of some headline-grabbing fiasco involving the world's greatest actor, my outward resolve finally needed the reinforcement of an inward stiff drink. And I needed a second when I discovered that the anxiety had gripped Olivier himself – he had retreated into Barry Johnston's office and stretched himself on the desk in darkness with a raincoat as a pillow. Nevertheless when the moment came he produced a fine performance, with all that familiar silvery style:

The spacious firmament on high,
With all the blue ethereal sky,
And spangled heav'ns, a shining frame,
Their great Original proclaim...

The poem brought our first night to an uplifting close and as the screen went dark a little after 11.30 p.m. all present sank into exhausted relief. We had done it, and once they caught their breath everyone else involved joined me in celebrating with gusto. A happy Olivier played his part too, signing many autographs and giving our youthful staff a tremendous boost.

6

Golden Days of Promise

If Ulster Television had not been a hit from day one then day two would have clinched it, for the Sunday line-up was exceptionally strong, including *Rich and Rare,* a programme about Northern Ireland made by Lord Wakehurst himself, a fine Armchair Theatre production of an Ulster play, Joe Tomelty's *A Shilling for the Evil Day,* and *Sunday Night at the London Palladium* featuring Cliff Richard, the Beverly Sisters and the Tiller Girls. It was hugely popular and proved beyond doubt that we could offer a rich alternative to the BBC. In the weeks and months that followed, the programme on which we had pinned so many hopes, *Roundabout,* steadily won the affections of the Ulster audience, while *Robin Hood* was only one of a number of series which 'hooked' people. *Emergency Ward 10, The Invisible Man, Highway Patrol* and *Rawhide* all proved highly successful, as did *Fury The Wonder Horse, The Flying Doctor* and *I Love Lucy*. On Mondays we had Michael Miles's *Double Your Money* and on Fridays Hughie Green's *Take Your Pick,* both infectious and addictive game shows. I had told myself when I took on the job that our success would be measured in terms of people discussing our shows in the bus or the street and in that we were richly rewarded, for it seemed that everybody was watching and absorbing UTV. The ratings confirmed this, showing that an astounding 85 per cent of people with sets were watching our programmes, with a peak of 96 per cent considered to be a world record.

The success of *Roundabout* was the most satisfying of all because it worked exactly as we wanted, putting us in touch with the people of Northern Ireland and putting them in touch with us. Anne Gregg and Ivor Mills, both young and attractive, hit it off with each other and the audience so the programme had real warmth to it. As for the guests, they were mostly people who had never expected to find themselves on television and the effect on them was almost magical. Some declined to have their make-up taken off and wore it down the street as they left, such was their pride. Others would offer to write a cheque after their moment of fame and express great surprise when told that we would pay them (the maximum fee was £1 a minute). This novelty factor brought problems too: in the early days the presenters were instructed to do a quick run-through with the guest but this was often misunderstood, so that once they were on air and the same questions came up the interviewee might say: 'But I told you that a minute ago...'

As an example of the sort of people who made it on to the programme, one interviewee was a man I had observed for years painting the railings along the side of the Lagan between Queen's Bridge and Stranmillis. It seemed an unending job. One day I engaged him in conversation and after an amusing chat I suggested that he should come on *Roundabout* the following week. Contrary to request, of course, he turned up in his best Sunday suit rather than his paint-spattered work clothes but there was nothing to be done about that so into the studio he went. I always watched from my office so that evening I settled down to enjoy Ivor Mills doing the interview and was just congratulating myself on an original idea when Ivor asked the inevitable question: was it ever boring, painting the same railings all year round? 'Of course it's fucking boring,' came the reply. My heart stopped. This was going out live. I rose from my desk, poured myself a stiff drink and waited for the storm, but it never came. We had stolen a march on Kenneth Tynan by broadcasting the F word, but no one rang; no one complained. I still don't know how we got away with it. In fact no one outside the company mentioned it to me until that weekend at the golf club, when a friend inquired: 'Did I by any chance hear a four-letter word on your programme the other night?' I adopted a tone of wounded incredulity. 'On Ulster Television? On my channel? A four-letter word?' The golfer beat a retreat, accepting that of course it was unthinkable.

Another *Roundabout* guest was a well-known oboe player who

was asked, naturally, how he came to take up the instrument. He began his answer: 'I was lying in bed one morning enjoying myself...' Had everybody kept a straight face we would have been fine, but to the musician's dismay the entire studio, including the interviewer, collapsed into giggles. The screen had to be blanked for a while to allow them to regain their composure. It is in the nature of live television that I remember such moments best, but mistakes were rare and the programme was well produced and very good viewing. It proved popular with visiting celebrities and in the first year we counted among our guests the director John Huston, the footballer Danny Blanchflower, the pianist Russ Conway, the Hollywood star Stephen Boyd (a Belfast man) and the singer Alma Cogan. Not for nothing did *Roundabout* routinely capture at least three-quarters of the Northern Ireland audience. It even won the grudging approval of the *Belfast Telegraph* and, as I have said, the formula was eventually copied in almost every television region in the country, both on ITV and BBC.

As we found our feet our minds turned to keeping promises. One early step in expanding homegrown output was to extend *Roundabout* to 40 minutes, while we also spun off a couple of features from the show as programmes in their own right – the Friday sports preview, for example, which Ernest Strathdee continued to present. The Board remained extremely cautious even though what they regarded as outrageously expensive was pretty low-budget even by the standards of the time, but almost despite them we found ways of making shows that were low in cost and high in value. Some of these left a lasting mark, and none more than *Romper Room*. This was American in origin and the UK rights were in the hands of Paul Talbot, the man behind many of the most popular quiz shows on both BBC and ITV. We were looking for a programme for pre-school children (I always liked the idea of catching the viewers young) and we felt that in Adrienne McGuill we had the perfect presenter, so when Paul came to Belfast the deal was quickly done and the show was rapidly on air. From then on Adrienne was 'Miss Adrienne' and for the rest of the 1960s weekday evenings began with 20 minutes of games and stories performed with and for a group of invited children. It was as charming as it was simple. Over the years thousands of children appeared on *Romper Room* and for very many of them – and their families – it was to be an enduring happy memory. Many still know the catchphrases – 'Magic mirror, tell me today…' and 'Romper, stomper, bomper, boo…' – and to this day I am greeted by people in their 40s who want to tell me their stories of Miss Adrienne or her successor Miss Helen. Some of them even expect me to recognise them from their childhood television appearances.

Besides *Romper Room* there was the inimitable *Tea Time With Tommy*. I had discovered Tommy James myself when visiting a Belfast shop to buy a piano for my wife and daughters. This cockney salesman from Mile End Road, I realized, was quite a character, with an effortless charm and a confident touch on the keys. Better than that he was a real entertainer. Tommy started with Ulster Television as a sort of general musical handyman, supplying a little tune here and there and advising on which recordings to use for backgrounds but eventually I persuaded our producers to give him his own show. The formula could not have been simpler: Tommy would read out a few short letters and requests from viewers – his postbag soon reached 100 letters a day – and then he and his trio would play some popular tunes. Birthdays and anniversaries were a speciality. He would have guests – the young Gloria Hunniford sang with him more than once, but there were also more established entertainers – and he kept up a brisk and friendly patter with them. The show lasted a little under half an hour and we used to record five every Saturday. Although a cruel joke did the rounds that 'he must be superstitious because he always plays the piano with his fingers crossed' Tommy proved extraordinarily popular. He was the local Hughie Green, probably our finest showbiz 'pro', in the best sense of the word.

Much more problematic than either of these – indeed nothing cost me more sleep or tested my powers of diplomacy more fully in the early years – was the introduction of a religious spot, known as *End the Day*. To be broadcast just before closedown, this was to involve a single clergyman delivering a short homily to viewers as they prepared to retire. The same person would appear each night for a week, so establishing some continuity and rapport with the public. From the remote distance of the 21st century this may seem a minor matter, even quaint, but things were different then. Religion was held to be a vital part of broadcasting and the ITA required all stations to do their bit. In Northern Ireland there were special circumstances: co-operation across the religious divide was extremely rare, and in the few places where it took place it was inevitably burdened with political implications. The apparently simple task of dividing up the *End the Day* slots between what were called the 'main streams of religion' – a task which fell to me – was therefore not simple. In other parts of the United Kingdom the broadcasts were divided between the denominations according to a formula based on a 13-week timetable, but this formula did not fit the religious profile of Northern Ireland. The Catholic Church had the largest following, with the Church of Ireland and Presbyterians close behind, followed by Methodists and others. I juggled the numbers in my head: 5:4:3:1 was likely to offend all the Protestant denominations; 4:4:4:1 would probably upset the Catholics; 5:3:3:2 would please nobody. I was close to desperation when, lying in the bath one night, inspiration struck. To extend the framework over the whole year, comprising 52 weeks, would give the flexibility needed. On this basis I proposed the following balance: 16 weeks for the Catholic Church; 15 for the Church of Ireland; 15 for the Presbyterian Church and six for the Methodists and others. To my great relief it proved acceptable to all, even the 'others' – Baptists, Jews and smaller churches – to whom the Methodists were to show considerable generosity.

While this was being resolved we had the job of introducing our prospective religious performers to the techniques of broadcasting and this brought anxieties of its own. We set up a series of seminars and because of the numbers involved we did them church by church. As luck would have it, of course, the Catholic session went disastrously wrong. Our 'pupils' gathered in the rehearsal room on the day and I gave the introductory talk, with a little history of the company, an outline of our plans and prospects and a timetable for the day. I explained that as soon as I finished talking to them the television by my side would come on and 'the very distinguished Mr S.E. Reynolds' would appear on closed circuit, explaining and illustrating a few 'dos and don'ts'. Unfortunately at the appointed moment the set failed to work and when a second set was carried in and hooked up it too remained blank. Knowing as I did that the Catholic clergy had their doubts about our new station, and conscious that this was hardly impressing them, I chose the path of firm leadership. I announced that I was dissatisfied and that I would now summon no less a person than our chief engineer, who would undoubtedly resolve matters forthwith. In came Frank Brady with yet another television and he set about connecting it up. When eventually he pressed the 'On' button, however, there was a loud crack and that screen too died stone dead, upon which Frank, loud and clear enough for every single person present to hear, uttered the single word 'Fuck!' It was a chilling moment. Fortunately, thanks to the mollifications of the charming 'S.E.', and also to the good manners of the men in dog collars (who, no doubt, had heard the word before) we survived this unhappy introduction. S.E. and I were taken out for a very pleasant lunch, good relations were cemented and the Catholic clergy went on to play their full part in launching *End the Day*.

This is not the place to list all our programmes from the 1960s or all those others we brought to Northern Ireland from the ITV network which became part of the collective folklore but there is one more in each of those categories of which I am particularly proud. The first is *Midnight Oil*, a pioneering adult education series which has a real claim to have been the earliest British forerunner of the Open University. This had been one of those 'aspirations' cooked up in the bidding period – William MacQuitty had the broad idea and provided the title – but I remained keen and some time in 1961 I set it in motion with the help of Michael Grant, then Vice-Chancellor of Queen's University. We gathered together a group of seven professors whom I knew and thought capable of performing on television, and proposed that each of them deliver six simple lectures introducing viewers to his subject – law, medicine, economics and so forth. They were keen, although there was almost a hiccup over money. One of them happened to be a member of our Board of whom I had cause to despair (we will meet him again in a moment) and perhaps inevitably it was he who asked what we would pay for these lectures. Equally inevitably he was the only one who thought £1 per minute insufficient, but he soon shut up when I suggested he should raise his anxieties at the next Board meeting (of course he never did). In the end everybody did a magnificent job. The 42 programmes went out after 10.30pm over the summer months of 1962 and were a resounding success, prompting one viewer to offer my favourite critical judgement of all – *Midnight Oil*, he declared, was 'useless to nobody'.

The other programme I want to mention is *Coronation Street*, merely to point out that when it first appeared in 1960 only two ITV stations carried it: the makers, Granada, and Ulster Television. I had liked it from the moment I heard of it – the idea of a soap opera set in a single terrace of houses with shops and pub – and I thought that Northern Ireland people, and particularly Belfast people, would find it easy to identify with such a setting. We supported *Coronation Street* from the start, the viewers loved it and we shared in its success in more ways than one.

Things were looking up on the business side too, which was just as well given the attitudes of some on the Board. Pessimism and personal antipathies were not our only problems in that department; we also had far too many directors (18), which caused needless debate and back-biting. One Board member took a delight in painstaking scrutiny of Barry Johnston's accounts, querying the tiniest sums and loftily challenging the accounting methods used. When Lord Antrim politely pointed out that the sums all added up he answered that he 'did not count that way' and ploughed on. Poor Sir Francis Evans would sit through this with an inscrutable expression, tearing sheets of paper into ever-tinier pieces until his ashtray was filled with minute confetti – perhaps a hangover from his diplomatic days shredding secret documents. Another member of the Board was the Queen's professor mentioned above, who had been recruited to provide intellectual gloss but when, for example, the chairman sought his comments after our first week on air he replied: 'My Lord, the programmes are not too bad but why do we have to have those dreadful advertisements?'

Even the most blinkered or gloomy director soon had to admit that not only had we avoided bankruptcy but we were set fair for handsome profits. Those 'dreadful advertisements' were rolling in, indeed we were riding something of a wave. So impressive were our ratings and so good at his job was ABC's Michael Hutcheson that more and more national advertisers were including us in their campaigns. Our popular success, moreover, meant that more and more people in Northern Ireland were buying television sets, which in turn led to increased revenue from the advertisements we carried. It was a virtuous upward spiral. All of this gave me the confidence, despite doubts on the Board, to end the advertising arrangement with ABC – the contract now favoured them more than us – and to set up our own small sales office on the Marylebone Road in London. Happily Mike agreed to join us and he was to remain in charge there for many years as well as becoming a close and good friend. In Northern Ireland, meanwhile, Basil Lapworth was winning over the local business community – and that did not just mean Belfast. I recall joining a meeting between Basil and the boss of a prominent creamery who was considering advertising with us. Both were fairly well oiled after a good lunch – but in businesslike mood. A deal was soon struck and a sum agreed – in the region of £1,000 – prompting the client to plunge his hand into his pocket and produce an enormous roll of banknotes secured by a rubber band. Slowly he counted out the appropriate sum into Basil's hand and then peeled off two extra fivers, presenting one to Basil and one to me. 'There's your luck pennies,' he said, and with that he spat on his hand and we shook. They remained good advertisers for years.

Cyril Lord, the carpet magnate, was another key customer and that relationship also began unconventionally. One Friday night he rang me at home to say he had job vacancies to fill urgently and could he have some of those '£5 for five seconds' advertisements he had been told about? I said yes and he dictated a script to me over the phone, telling me he wanted it transmitted several times that same weekend. We agreed a price and hung up. I could see that the script would have filled 20 seconds rather than five so I edited it down and it duly went out. Several of the 'spots' had been aired when Lord called me from his home, this time in a furious temper. What right had I, he demanded to know, to change his advertisement? I explained that the script had been far too long and when that failed to mollify him I stated firmly that we retained complete rights in such matters and if he had any complaints he could put them in writing. Equally firmly he said he would. First thing on the Monday, however, I received a third call from him, this time in a completely different mood. 'I got to the factory this morning,' he told me excitedly, 'and there was a long queue of people lining up for those jobs. I'll be using more of your commercials.' And so he did, rapidly progressing from the five-second slides to longer, more lavish (and for us much more profitable) filmed promotions.

It would be hard to exaggerate the impact of the advertisements, and it was clear that Northern Ireland had been badly 'under-advertised' before we came along. One of the big detergent companies saw its sales increase by 160 per cent in a few weeks thanks to a campaign on Ulster Television, and when a Belfast store announced a fur sale on our screens it saw a 300 per cent increase in business the next day. There was even some evidence that our arrival boosted growth across the whole of the local retail industry.

One happy result of this burgeoning success was that in autumn 1962 we were able to introduce news reports. This was underpinned by substantial investment: a second studio, much bigger than the first, was equipped and opened, film cameras and processing equipment were bought and journalists and editors were recruited to supply the content. The new service was announced with great fanfare in *TV Post*, accompanied by a picture of a new camera atop a handsome Morris Minor van in company livery. Every weekday from then on we opened transmission at 4.40 p.m. with a five-minute local news bulletin. At 6.05 p.m. there was another bulletin and then, after *Teatime with Tommy*, came *Newsview*, a revamped and punchier version of *Roundabout* with a stronger news element. Anne Gregg had moved to Anglia Television and the show was presented by Ivor Mills and Ernest Strathdee, with Jimmy Greene reading the bulletins. I was delighted with this new string to our bow although I had no idea how important it was to become.

I can't let Anne Gregg go without recalling another point of pride, which was that so much of our talent from those early days went on to considerable achievement. Her success is well known and was all the more satisfying since it so eloquently refuted the view often expressed at the time of our launch that we were wrong to use a woman, and a teenager at that, on a programme such as *Roundabout*. Ivor, too, was to become nationally known alongside Reginald Bosanquet and Sandy Gall at ITN, while on the production side Derek Bailey, who directed *Midnight Oil* among other programmes, went on to national and international success as an award-winning director on the arts programme *Aquarius*. I have mentioned Gloria Hunniford, to whom we gave important breaks, but two other household names who owed something to *Roundabout* or *Teatime with Tommy* were Val Doonican - he made his first television appearance on Ulster Television for the regulation £5 for five minutes - and Roger Whitaker. The latter, though he was no Irishman, was spotted in a Belfast pub by our first programme director, John Scholz Conway, who suggested that I should come along for a drink and hear him sing. We quickly signed him up and recorded a series of 13 shows which were our first sales to the network and which launched him to international fame. Neither he nor Val ever forgot where they started and they remained good friends to Ulster Television even at the height of their fame.

In financial terms our success was crowned when Ulster Television was floated on the Stock Exchange in 1961. This was arranged by the sagacious and well-connected George Cameron, who recruited the City firm of Lazard Brothers as advisers. I recall some amusement in our boardroom when we learned that Lazards' had assigned a Mr Wylie to handle the affair and that he would be assisted by one Lord Tryon. Despite their pantomime names they and George did a fine job and when the shares reached the market our initial investors found they had £30 for every £1 they had originally put in. All the early doubts and squabbling were exposed as foolish and short-sighted. It was a glittering return, testimony not only to staff effort and successful management but also to the huge commercial appeal of ITV and to the advertising boom into which we had launched. This was the time when Roy Thomson of STV remarked that commercial television was 'a licence to print money', a glib phrase hung around ITV's neck through good years and bad. It was rather less true of Ulster Television than of STV and some of the bigger companies, where the return on investment was not 30 to one but sometimes 500 to one and even 1,000 to one.

What did all this success mean for me? On one level it is easy to imagine. Still in my early 30s and with previous experience only in newspapers, I had joined – not without hesitation – an embryonic company in deep crisis, and in 18 months we had created a dazzlingly successful business by the standards of Northern Ireland. I started, no doubt, as a doubtful quantity in the eyes of the directors, but I was able to convince them – or at least those who mattered – that I had the flair, drive and nous to make the company work, so when William MacQuitty fulfilled his promise to step aside I became Managing Director. Though Ulster Television was and always would be the work of many hands (and I have mentioned only a handful of the many who distinguished themselves) I had become the boss with all the responsibilities and satisfactions that brought. The job was everything I had imagined: I could draw on my experience both in the theatre and in newspapers; I could indulge a new-found taste for publicity; I could negotiate and make big deals and I could tackle new problems and have new ideas every day. On top of that I was pretty well paid at £3,500 a year and had proved something important to myself. Our family tradition, going back well over a century to Sir James, his father James Alexander and beyond, is this business now called 'the media'. I may have been a younger son but here I was, in the early 1960s, riding the crest of the television wave, the most exciting development around, and with a show that – at least in my less humble moments – I could call my own.

Unfortunately running Ulster Television turned out to be a 24-hour-a-day assignment leaving room for very little else, and for this I was to pay a heavy price. I was coming home late at night with briefcases full of papers and sitting like an automaton for hours, reading, noting and dictating as well as making and taking phone calls, and only looking up to watch the screen. More and more, too, work was taking over my social life, for the television and advertising worlds were notoriously geared towards eating, drinking and late nights. Such relaxing as I did was usually work-related: representing the company, making contacts, glad-handing and sealing deals over long dinners. Then in the mornings I was up and out early, heading for Havelock House and the new day's business. Often I was in London or abroad, for as we shall see the job entailed a great deal of politicking in the wider television world. This was not a life for a young husband and father. Perhaps it wasn't quite as bad as I have painted it but it must have seemed that way to my wife Joy and to my dear daughters. For this and other reasons my marriage hit the rocks in the early 1960s just as the company blossomed. We parted briefly, were reconciled and then, after six more years, parted again for good. By the end, in 1967 there was rancour on both sides and the divorce process – no simple matter in those days – was extremely testing.

7
American Interlude

There have been various passions in my life and one of these is the United States. I had no family or business connections there but I had a fascination born in early visits to the cinema and cultivated throughout my education, culminating in the study of the American Revolution under Professor Moody at Trinity. In 1962 I finally went there and instantly fell for the place and its people, and for that first introduction, an unexpected and exciting interlude in my career, I have the U.S. State Department to thank. They run a scholarship programme which takes a selection of up-and-coming young people from around the world, shows them the United States and gives them an impression of what makes it tick. The idea, I assume, is that some of the beneficiaries will become people of influence in their own countries and that they will then have ready-made American knowledge and contacts to help them. In 1962 I was asked to take part in that year's programme and not surprisingly I jumped at the chance. This was 40 years ago and travel to the United States was nothing like as easy or as common as it is today, so the prospect of the trip alone was thrilling. The prospect of access to opinion-formers of all kinds and to the U.S. television and movie industries in particular was a sensational bonus. I knew, nevertheless, that our Board would be somewhat less excited at the idea of their young chief executive departing for eight weeks. And worse still, since the scholarship package was modest (though it included free flights and various 'pledges' of hospitality, but only $20 a day for expenses) I would not only need their blessing but also some cash from the well-guarded company coffers. I answered that since the station was going well I could be spared and that it was a golden opportunity for the company to make contacts in, and to learn from, the country which led the world in commercial television. After a good deal of humming and hawing they gave their approval and, with characteristic munificence, voted the grand sum of £100 for the whole trip.

The adventure began on 5th November 1962 with a first-class TWA flight from London when, for the first time, I had that odd experience of flying over Belfast on the way to America. On arrival in New York (where the airport was still called Idlewild) I was met by two State Department officials who even then showed concern at greeting somebody from Northern Ireland – I assume because the IRA had only recently been active. I must have passed muster because, after an indoctrination session at the Ambassador's Club, I was sent on to Washington to meet the people who would arrange my tour, Bill Hadley Jnr and his assistant Nancy Buttermark. Over the next day or two, while they worked on the schedule for my whistlestop tour around the U.S.A., I visited the great monuments of the American capital in the day and in the evenings watched their very different brand of television. Besides seeing several programmes which soon afterwards became household staples in Britain, I watched Johnny Carson in the *Tonight* show for his, and my, first time. I also scrutinized their local news programmes and remember feeling that, for all the money and technology lavished on them, they were no better than *Roundabout*.

From Washington I went to Boston – a raw, cold place in November – where I visited Harvard, was suitably impressed and then found myself marooned for the Thanksgiving holiday. Fortunately I fell upon the hospitality of the Irish consul, Con Howard, a friendly figure who was to crop up many times in my subsequent career. It may have been his wish to steer Ulster Television into greener fields than political balance allowed. My next stop was New York, where I stayed in a hotel recently vacated by the young Fidel Castro and his entourage, in town to address the United Nations. I remember being struck by the bad roads in the city – a surprise in a place supposed to be a sort of El Dorado. The way to see New York, unlike Washington, was on foot. I visited the television companies, who were most welcoming. ABC, then led by

Leonard Goldensen, was the coming third force in those days, able to poach the best talent from CBS and NBC, and they gave me a glimpse of the shape of television to come. They were planning several powerful Western and crime series in which each show would last an hour rather than the half-hour which was then the norm. Before long these enabled ABC to steal a march on their rivals and soon after that they became the staples of prime time television the world over. At CBS I remember a fascinating couple of days watching coverage of the mid-term elections then taking place. I saw everything from the close-of-polls bulletin through the analysis of breaking results (which I watched on the studio floor) to the newsroom post-mortem the next evening. I vividly recall the formidable Bill Leonard, a legend among newsmen, chairing the last of these. Far from being a wallow in self-congratulation it was a bracing affair with criticisms aired and no feelings spared. Half-way through it Leonard abruptly left the chair saying only that he would 'be back in a couple of minutes'; moments later I saw his face appear on a silent screen in a corner of the room – he was on air again, delivering another live commentary to the nation – and then, as swiftly as he had disappeared, he was back among us, in the chair again as if nothing important had intervened.

Besides the work involved, one of the joys of the scholarship programme was the succession of distinguished people roped in on promises to act as patrons. In New York I struck lucky, for thanks to a former U.S. ambassador to France not only was I briefly made an honorary member of the Racquets Club – a venerable but welcoming institution – but was also given a supply of free stalls tickets to the best shows on Broadway. So it was that I saw *Camelot* with Vanessa Redgrave, *A Funny Thing Happened on the Way to the Forum* with Zero Mostel, and *How To Succeed In Business Without Really Trying* with Robert Morse. The UTV Board back in Belfast would have been scandalized by how much I was enjoying myself but, despite appearances, I was not in the lap of luxury for the important gap in the scholarship arrangements was apparent. Flights, travel, meetings and much else were laid on with great style but square meals were few and my meagre means were not sufficient to cover hotel costs and keep me properly fed. I learned to eat whatever free food came my way, scoffing cocktail sausages and sandwiches at official receptions (while trying all the time to keep up a proper flow of small talk) and shamelessly exploiting the Happy Hour at local bars, where one beer came with all the nibbles one could eat. This was hardly enough, so while my mind feasted in the land of plenty my body was subjected to an unwelcome fast.

One patron in New York introduced me to a particularly thrilling new aspect of American commuter life. He lived in the elegant suburb of Scarsdale and on the way from the railway station to his house we pulled into the car park of a supermarket where he told me he was going to 'do the weekly shop' – a phrase new to me. In Northern Ireland that word 'supermarket', if it was used at all in those days, meant at best a small shop that boasted the novelty of being self-service. In America supermarkets as big as warehouses in their own sprawling car parks were already a feature of the suburbs and I watched in wonder as my host did all his shopping in 20 minutes flat, loading it all effortlessly into the 'trunk' of his car. It was so convenient and such good value that I was bowled over. The experience of being taken to supermarkets was to be repeated several times in the course of my American trip and I was so impressed that on my return to Belfast I wrote a paper for our Board suggesting that Ulster Television should get into this business immediately. My idea was that we should go into partnership with an established retailer, taking a stake in return for regular advertising. Alas, the Board did not see it my way, but supermarkets soon took off without us, the first being 'Supermac', established by Anderson & McAuley in south-east Belfast.

I bought one item in that Scarsdale supermarket and it was a new shirt, for by that stage I was already in short supply of clean clothes. Hotel laundries were way beyond my means so, to put it tastefully, I was getting the full wear out of my limited wardrobe. By the time I reached Chicago, the next stop after New York, the problem had grown into a full-blown, almost malodorous, crisis, so I bought a packet of detergent, threw shirts, socks and underclothes into the bath in my hotel room, added powder and ran the taps. Unfortunately, like many men unfamiliar with these things I greatly overdid the soap so that, long before the bath was full, brilliant white suds were streaming from the bathroom on to my bedroom floor. Taken by surprise – I was naked at the time – I grabbed a towel and began to herd the bubbles back to whence they came. This had little effect and soon the suds were oozing out under my door into the hotel corridor. Suddenly the door burst open and a large, black chambermaid stood on the threshold wearing an expression of the greatest astonishment. For a moment she surveyed the scene of destruction – bubbles everywhere and me stark naked in the middle – and then she burst out laughing. When she had recovered her composure and I had covered my modesty with the towel I explained my predicament and my blunder, and she could not have been more helpful. Wiping away tears of laughter, she told me: 'Man, I would have done them for you for nothing.' The laundry problem, none the less, persisted and in another hotel later in my trip I was obliged to repeat the bath experiment, this time encountering a different problem. As I carried the box through reception in an airline bag it leaked, and the result was a neat trail of powder leading across the lobby to the lift, and from the lift door on my floor along the various corridors to my room. Not only had I given myself away but had also given a great deal of amusement to the hotel staff.

Chicago conjures up two other memories. One was my visit to the offices of the local ABC television station, where the boss was a man called 'Red' Quinlan, from whom I learned a useful lesson. Chicago is a lively, volatile city and, in the effort to keep the community and its leaders happy, Quinlan invited groups of people into his station for lunch, then showed them around and afterwards set them down for a 'no holds barred' question and answer session. Politicians, business people and worthies of all kinds – some of them outspoken critics of the station – would turn up and the results, I learned, were extremely positive. This was another idea I brought home to Belfast and this time was able to put it into practice. Over the years – and especially when licence renewal was coming up – it proved a great way of gauging sentiment while at the same time 'selling' the company. Doubters could be won over, people who knew little of our work could be turned into admirers, anger could be vented and, once in a while, real 'enemies' could be flushed out into the open. Quinlan did me a great favour.

My other Chicago memory is of a radio appearance. Sometimes people on these State Department scholarships are treated like visiting VIPs, and so one evening I found myself booked on a chat show broadcast by a Chicago station. I was a little surprised when I turned up just ahead of the appointed hour and no one else was there but as the hour struck the place suddenly filled with people and we were on air. We talked happily for a while and then as my throat grew dry I asked for a drink whereupon a waiter appeared and served everyone. He returned several times during advertisement breaks, topping up glasses and even distributing sandwiches; so the evening grew steadily livelier. But when the show ended, after four hours of animated conversation ranging over the whole gamut of world affairs, the host and all the other guests vanished as suddenly as they had appeared and I was left alone to gather up my belongings. At this moment the waiter reappeared, presented me with a bar bill almost as long as he was tall and demanded that I pay it. I protested that I was not in charge of the show but it was only when I showed him my slender wallet and explained that as an impoverished foreign visitor I could not afford to pay him that he went to look for his money elsewhere. So much for being a VIP.

After Chicago it was San Francisco, where I received another, more uplifting, lesson in low-budget broadcasting – this time from an educational television station which was the absolute antithesis of the well-funded networks. They begged and borrowed programmes from other broadcasters to keep themselves on the air and never paid fees to visiting performers on the simple grounds that 'We have no money'. To this day I remember that the studio floor, instead of being the shining, perfectly level sheet of lino our engineers had insisted on having in Havelock House, was a rough-hewn concrete affair that dipped and rose so that a camera moving across it on wheels gave viewers the impression of being at sea. But these people were nothing if not resourceful. One of their visitors was the film star Kim Novak, a real sex symbol in those days, and some clever soul persuaded her to donate to the station a pair of sheets in which she had slept. These were then cut up, tailored into neckties and auctioned off to her admirers on air – the managers told me the stunt paid all their bills for a week.

Los Angeles, two-thirds road and one-third buildings, proved as weird as I could have hoped. I got an early taste of its values from one of the 'pledge' people who watched over me there, a charming, blue-rinsed old lady who, it turned out, owned a large downtown hotel. (Many of these good people, by the way, were elderly; I remember a doddery old couple who took me for a drive around San Francisco and ended up getting lost. They missed a turn near the Golden Gate Bridge and it was 20 miles later before we got back on track.) Anyway, my Los Angeles lady fed me dinner and then took me to see her hotel, which was a splendid edifice rising to about 15 storeys. When I remarked on how proud she must be to own it she shook her head and said: 'Oh no. I'm going to knock it down and turn it into a parking lot. That way I'll make serious money.' I soon discovered that the same kind of extravagant unpredictability – not to mention the same ruthless economics – ruled the Hollywood movie scene, which I was there to inspect. Several 'big wheels' agreed to see me but none of them conformed remotely to expectations. One in particular welcomed me to his office at 9 a.m. and remained on the phone more or less continuously until 4 p.m., leaving me to drink Scotch, eavesdrop and talk to his secretaries. When he finally hung up and caught my eye he thrust his hand out and announced: 'It has been wonderful visiting with you Mr Henderson; you really are a very interesting person.' Then he took his leave. Observing my mystification, one of his flunkeys tried to make it up by whisking me off to a club in the red light district where I witnessed pole dancing for the first time, so some might say the day was not entirely wasted. My other encounters with studio executives had the same near-miss quality and what I really remember them for is the entourages. Each big name came with a retinue of lawyers and agents and other dogsbodies who seemed to do all the talking and thinking for him and it was impossible to have a sensible conversation or to discover what talents might have got this famous person to the top.

Far better value were the writers, although they were often treated like cattle. One who was not was the television writer David Dortort, creator of the Western series *Bonanza,* whom I met at the NBC studios in Burbank. He was not only the sole writer on the series but was also the producer, and I found him sitting at a desk with an immense pad of paper before him and a stack of well-sharpened pencils. He explained to me coolly that shooting was going on even as we were speaking and that his script was only slightly ahead of the running plot – sure enough, somebody came in while I was there to collect a fresh bundle of lines for the actors. It seemed a nightmarish way to proceed, guaranteed to keep everybody under terrible pressure, but Dortort told me with a laugh that it was for the benefit of the actors: 'These guys can't carry much in their heads so I write it out for them just ahead of time.' He went on to offer another explanation, however, which had more of a ring of truth: so long as the next scene existed in his head alone, he said, 'the guys upstairs' could not sack him. Crazy or not, the system worked, for this was an operation of awesome efficiency. Dortort produced the words single-handed; there was just a handful of actors; the sets were basic in the extreme and the technicians were almost all men of advanced years taking refuge from the movie industry. Yet this lean team produced 39 ratings-topping episodes of *Bonanza* each year without fail, and the remaining 13 weeks were spent filming location shots in the desert, recharging batteries and taking those very short American summer holidays. I was impressed.

From Los Angeles I travelled to Memphis, Tennessee, of which my principal memory is great plumes of smoke filling the horizon – the corn harvest, it was explained, had been too good and they were burning off the surplus. Here at once was vivid evidence of the huge productive power of the United States and of its sometimes grotesque wastefulness – at that time, after all (as at any other time), there were people starving somewhere in the world. After Memphis came Houston, Texas, and a dizzying round of breakfasts, lunches and dinners given by the Rotary and the Chamber of Commerce, at several of which I was required to speak. I have a vague recollection of firing myself up with brandy eggnogs for a speech at a 6.45 a.m. breakfast and then having a haircut and a snooze in the park before addressing another audience at lunch. Lord knows what I told them all. I do remember a tour of the rich Houston suburbs which led to an extraordinary discovery. As we turned down a street of mansions I noticed that, unlike any other street we had seen, half the properties were for sale. I was told that a black family had just moved in, their home apparently bought with the help of the National Association for the Advancement of Coloured People as a political initiative. Half the local white householders, my guide informed me, were responding by selling up. It seemed a strange business and proof of an unhappy state of affairs, but the memory of that row of 'For Sale' signs always brings to my mind the story of the black American doctor who moved with his family into a well-off white district. He was out weeding his flower beds on the first Saturday morning when a neighbour spotted him and, misreading the situation, inquired how much he was paid as a gardener. 'I gets no money,' came the reply, 'but I gets to sleep with the lady of the house.'

New Orleans and Miami followed and then it was back to New York and, eventually, home. Besides the above I had toured the offices of the *Washington Post*, climbed the Statue of Liberty, descended by donkey into the Grand Canyon and survived a late-night poker school in New Orleans. I met Stanley Holloway on the set of *My Fair Lady* and Red Skelton on the set of a whisky commercial, and I met ordinary Americans of all kinds, classes and colours – on planes, in taxis, in bars and hotels, offices and shops. In just over eight weeks I think I saw and did as much as was possible and I found the place and its people utterly enthralling. One strange thing I will always remember: these were the days of John F. Kennedy's presidency, the 'Camelot' period, as it has been called, which came before his assassination a year later. Yet in all my journeys and all my conversations I scarcely heard a word spoken in his favour. Perhaps these were 'mid-term blues', but the absence of affection was striking.

It should be little wonder that an experience such as this left its mark on me, both personally and professionally. Personally, I was left with an enduring regard for the United States and I have always loved going back, while professionally the trip was a powerful stimulant. I had travelled in Europe before but this was something else – America at its most dynamic and optimistic, full of creative buzz and bustle. Here was I, running a small commercial television company on the fringe of the United Kingdom, and I had witnessed at first hand the operations of ABC, NBC and CBS as well as Hollywood production studios and small-time local stations. I had interviewed senior executives and creative people and observed the latest technology and the latest production techniques. It was a glimpse into the future, into another decade, and it filled me with ideas and made me more ambitious than ever for Ulster Television and ITV. Of course there were things I didn't like – the naked commercialism of American television and the ruthless pursuit of ratings – but I found much that I liked. Some of what I learned would emerge in the way I ran things, and some in the programmes we produced.

The most obvious effect was on programme ideas. We produced two historical series, *Ulster and America* and later the more lavish *God's Frontiersmen*, celebrating Ulster's links with America and in particular that generation of Ulstermen who emigrated to the American colonies in the eighteenth century and played leading parts in the War of Independence. On the death of John F. Kennedy in 1963 we ditched our whole schedule and produced an evening of tributes to the man, including a personal commentary and reminiscence by the U.S. consul in Belfast. And years later, on the American bicentenary in 1976, I threw caution to the winds and

Americanized the station for a whole week, bringing in American announcers, raiding the archives for factual material and producing a whole string of special programmes. Two shows I remember were an account of the big U.S. companies then active in Northern Ireland, notably Dupont and Hughes, and a major interview with my old Trinity friend the American novelist J.P. Donleavy, author of *The Ginger Man* and denizen of a castle near Mullingar. One thing we did not do, because we were not allowed to, was to exceed the dreary quota of 14 per cent American entertainment content that was set by the ITA.

And, as we will see, my romance with America was still only beginning.

8

No Two Days the Same

Back in Belfast, although the new station was established and successful, my life as managing director in the mid-1960s was anything but settled. Television is a mercurial mistress and every day her demands are different. On the programme side each new venture tested creativity and stamina, particularly as I was always restless – I felt it was important never to stand still and never to allow a formula to become stale. I worked, too, to build up our advertising base and publicize our achievements, while at Havelock House there were always budgets to be managed, people to be recruited, personnel difficulties to be dealt with – and labour problems to be handled.

A huge amount of my time was taken up by the jousting with trade unions which was a feature of all industry in those days but which was especially persistent and tiresome in television. I had no previous experience in this field and had to learn fast. It began even before we went on air, when we received a visit from the labour relations adviser to the ITV companies. He advised us, as he advised all the new companies, to sign the existing national agreements with the television trade unions and, after long debate among ourselves, we did so. It was a decision we came to regret. ITV was dominated in those days by companies with substantial interests in the film industry – Granada, for example, through the Bernsteins, and ABC through its connection with Warner Brothers – and they had earlier agreed to concede in television the sort of labour arrangements established in the 'gravy days' of British film. This may have bought peace in the short term but it was a long-term recipe for trouble at ITV because, although television and film may *seem* similar, in practice they are very different. Films are one-off projects involving irregular hours and days, location changes and short-term contracts, and the film technicians naturally sought to protect themselves from the resulting uncertainties. Their pay and conditions were thus very generous by most standards. Television, by contrast, was stable, regular employment with little risk and no temporary lay-offs and so similar pay and practices were not appropriate, yet that was precisely what the national agreements guaranteed. Granada, ABC and the others had accepted this because it was what they knew, and because they did not want to rock the film boat.

Practices thus took root at Ulster Television which, looking back, appear absurd. For example, technicians who worked 'unusual' hours were entitled to extra pay. Fair enough, you might say, and if we had to keep people busy into the small hours on top of a normal day's work I happily agreed, but that was rarely the case. Naturally the technicians worked in the evenings – that was when we broadcast - but in the early years the station was routinely off the air and everybody on their way home before we reached the midnight threshold for these extra payments. Nevertheless, if a broadcast overran or was extended, then there was a risk that the last technician might still be on the premises at the stroke of midnight and if that happened he was entitled not only to overtime but also to his 'unsocial hours' bonus. Very often there were further complications, because if he worked past midnight and was required to work again before the following midnight, the extra payment would have to be higher, and if that extra few minutes took him into the weekend it would be higher still. For these few minutes, therefore, a technician might have to be paid four or even five times the usual rate for the whole eight hours. It does not take a cynic to see that, with a 40 hour bonus at stake, technicians had a powerful vested interest in arranging for those extra minutes. Since we had a tightly-controlled operation (for example we spent only £20 per programme on *Roundabout*, excluding fixed costs) we found efficiency, trust and all-round fairness hard to maintain. We kept a close eye on the clock and on several occasions I actually pulled the plug on a programme to ensure that everybody was out of Havelock House on time. There were occasions, however, when this was not possible and the extra minutes on air prompted big payments. Not only did this cost heavily but it also caused jealousies and tensions among the other staff, even among members of the same union, which could sometimes sour the whole atmosphere at Havelock House.

In the fat years, the years of Roy Thomson's famous 'license to print money', few questions were raised about these 'restrictive practices' as they later came to be known. The unions saw it as their way of getting a bigger share of the profits of the new industry while many managements were naïve enough not to complain. But it was illogical and unjust, especially for Ulster Television, which existed in a small, distinct local economy where the cost of living was lower than the rest of the United Kingdom. It didn't make sense for us to pay these rates and although some people did well out of the arrangements it was at the cost of constant bickering – I often felt I was living in the Peter Sellers world of *I'm All Right Jack*. It also limited the company's ability to expand, make more programmes and create more jobs. I used to dread what would happen if the going got tougher for ITV, but even I did not foresee how shambolic it would be, and how destructive to creativity and friendly working relations.

Matters came to a head as the unions insisted on maintaining the upward march of pay and perks through the mid-1960s. Suddenly a curious paradox came into play, for although there were national agreements and although the unions involved were national organizations, they contrived to 'pick off' the companies one by one, doing separate deals. Often they did this in competition, so that when a union branch at one company saw a branch at another company winning better terms it would immediately seek to match them. The companies, for their part, allowed this to happen, sometimes because they too imagined they could come to more favourable terms in local deals. The inevitable consequence was that they did worse deals, union power increased and practices became even more restrictive. For the smaller, regional companies, strapped to the national agreements but deserted by the 'big four or five' when things went wrong, the consequences could be grim and we often lost both on the swings and on the roundabouts. We formed a regional group in an attempt to give ourselves more muscle and reluctantly I became the chief negotiator, trying (often in vain) to stiffen the resolve of the largest companies – I remember occasions when labour matters had me shuttling back and forth to London three times in one week. It did not help us that the Wilson government of the time wanted to meddle; on one occasion Lord Goodman intervened in a dispute ostensibly to bring peace but in effect to hand victory to the unions. No one could reject a 'deal' personally brokered by Harold Wilson's *eminence grise*.

Barring a small minority our own staff at Ulster Television were not especially militant; it was just that in national matters they were too few to have much influence over union decisions. I tried to maintain healthy working relations in Havelock House, for example by entertaining the shop stewards to drinks in my office at the end of every week, which kept things informal and nipped little problems in the bud. Once in the 1960s, when the ITV companies managed to unite briefly in the face of union demands, there was a full-blown national strike and Ulster Television employees were called out on to picket lines. Most of them reluctantly felt they had to comply while I decided that the management had an obligation to keep the station on the air. We were remarkably successful: a dozen of us, including several qualified engineers, not only maintained a flow of films and tapes but also put out a half-hour live evening programme. We kept this up for five days and then, to save union face locally, I let the screens go blank at the weekend. Later, when we had another strike, an improvised national television service was maintained in a similar way from ATV studios in Foley Street, London. I visited them there and found a motley crew of managers and advertising people enthusiastically working two to a machine – an ironic instance of overmanning. Although that strike ended in an acceptable deal the lesson was never learned and time and time again companies were taken to the cleaners because they lacked the nerve for a fight or because they still thought they could do clever deals on their own. The London companies in particular were offenders. It was only when the 1980s arrived, bringing new technology and a completely new political climate, that change came.

If trench warfare with the unions was an inescapable burden of my job, then friendly diplomacy across the border with the Republic was one of its pleasures. One of the many ways in which Ulster Television was unique in the ITV system was that it rubbed shoulders with a commercial station not ruled by the ITA. Radio Telefis Eireann, or RTE, was not on the air as a television station when we launched but it was already more than a twinkle in the eye of the Dublin government, and in both London and Belfast there was official concern about what this might mean. Would the signal from Dublin reach into Northern Ireland, even into Belfast? Would it be addressed to the nationalist population? This was technically possible (even though it would breach the European Broadcasting Union agreements to which RTE was a signatory) but what concerned me was not the political but the commercial threat, which could take a number of shapes. By the ITA's decree, for example, we were only allowed to show a limited number of the American series which were most popular with viewers at that time but RTE would be free of such restrictions. If they employed high-powered transmitters and packed their schedules with these shows there was a distinct danger that they might, as I put it at the time, 'blast Ulster Television off the air'. I resolved to do what I could to prevent this.

Visiting Dublin to attend an advertising industry lunch at the Metropole Hotel (a regular haunt of mine in my student years), I took the occasion to make discreet contact with Maurice Gorham, then the director-general of Radio Eireann. I suggested a rendezvous on O'Connell Bridge because I wanted an off-the-record meeting with none of the politicians and civil servants who would be certain to complicate matters. Maurice, intrigued by this Le Carre-style approach, duly arrived and with the Dublin traffic roaring by and the Liffey flowing quietly beneath I made my pitch. I suggested that a 'good neighbour' relationship between RTE and Ulster Television was in the interests of both parties and the people they served, and that in order to achieve this Ulster Television would promise never to seek an audience in the Republic nor to sell advertising on the basis of any cross-border 'overspill' from our transmitters. In return I sought an informal agreement that RTE would do the same. After some reflection, but with evident pleasure, Maurice pronounced this to be the course dictated by common sense and we had a deal. That gentleman's agreement struck on O'Connell Bridge stood for many years. We always had an overspill in the Republic, particularly down the east coast (in fact we sometimes received complaints from Dubliners about the weakness of our signal) but those viewers were never included in our audience figures. It was only in the closing days of my time at Ulster Television that the idea of formally claiming an audience in the Republic surfaced again, and even then I resisted it. Nor did RTE invade our airspace or our market.

The job of getting RTE on air was not given to Maurice Gorham but to a tall American, Ed Roth, who was seconded from NBC in New York. He was ably supported by Michael Barry, a former head of drama at the BBC, and by Jack White, previously of the *Irish Times*. Setting up home in what soon became luxurious new buildings in Donnybrook, south Dublin, they were in touch with us from the outset and a warm relationship developed. Many of their staff came to Havelock House to be trained, and Roth himself paid us a visit, arriving in a limousine which put my own more modest transport to shame. He was a taciturn fellow so after I had shown him the building I decided to introduce him to some of our viewers, of a kind he was unlikely to have encountered before – we adjourned to the Klondyke Bar in Sandy Row for what was a successful and, for him, revealing afternoon. Six months later he returned the compliment in rather different style, inviting my wife Joy and me to attend RTE's opening night on 31st December 1961, an impressive affair at which we sat next to Eamonn Andrews. Through the years that followed RTE had a succession of director generals, all whom became friends of mine, and happily whoever was in charge the same good relationship survived.

It was only threatened on two or three occasions, and then it was by meddling politicians. In the early years of the Troubles some well-meaning people would sometimes suggest that one solution might be to create an all-Ireland broadcasting company. This, they thought, would have the advantage of carrying the same message to everyone, whatever their politics or religion. What that message might be they would never say, but we at Ulster Television were always sure it would be less even-handed and not more. Occasionally these ideas found an ear in Dublin or London and we were required to challenge them, and one of these occasions involved an old Trinity friend, Conor Cruise O'Brien. Having made glittering careers in diplomacy and academia since leaving college, Conor turned to politics and in the 1970s was Minister for Post and Telegraphs in Dublin. Someone persuaded him that it would be a good idea if the RTE signal could be boosted to cover the whole of Northern Ireland and he put the idea to the London government in the hope that it would agree as a gesture to the nationalist community. Seeing the threat to our business and the likely damage to be caused by a service that would not be subject to the same constraints of fairness, I lobbied hard against this. It was around this time that I appeared with Conor on an RTE discussion programme on a different matter and I remember a long debate with him afterwards as I tried to give him a different view of Northern Ireland to the one which he had learned in his days at the Irish Department of Foreign Affairs. Fortunately that plan for an all-Ireland RTE, like all similar schemes, was soon ditched and I am equally happy to say that Conor's views eventually also changed. (Conor, incidentally, is a great wit. Shortly after he lost both his place in the Dublin Cabinet and his seat in the Dail I heard him speaking at a bibulous dinner in Oxford, where someone took exception to a remark of his. 'Cheap joke!' cried the heckler, to which Conor instantly replied: 'They're the only ones I can afford these days.')

Another piece of cross-border diplomacy arose from our good relations with the Catholic church. In the early 1960s I was approached on their behalf by Father Joe Dunn – who later became producer of *Radharc* for RTE – for help and advice on television facilities at the new Catholic religious training centre in Booterstown, Dublin. As it happened, at that time we were replacing our original Marconi Vidicom cameras and I told him they were for sale. As Joe insisted that the centre had no money I offered a reduced price of £700 for the lot and the deal was done. Shortly afterwards, therefore, I was invited to Booterstown for the opening ceremony and there I found myself in a small but elite company almost entirely composed of bishops. There was a service in Latin during which I found myself doing almost everything at the wrong moment – standing when I should have been kneeling; singing when I should have been silent – and this was followed by refreshments. No sooner had a bishop placed an enormous Scotch in my hand than I was ushered into the presence of the Archbishop of Dublin, the very formidable John Charles McQuaid. Emboldened, perhaps, by the drink, and conscious of my Trinity tie, which he must have recognized, I seized the moment for a challenge. Had the time not come, I asked the archbishop, for him to lift his church's ban on Catholics attending Trinity? Reflecting for a moment, he replied: 'I might be in favour myself but the old ladies would have none of it.' It was a clever evasion and perhaps even true, although opinion in the wider Catholic population was undoubtedly less dogmatic – for decades, after all, there had been some Catholics, including religious ones, who ignored the ban. The hierarchy changed its line almost immediately after the death in 1972 of its uncompromising archbishop.

Much as Joe Dunn had come through the doors of Havelock House looking for help, so in 1965 I received a visit from the great Ulster artist William Conor, and it was the beginning of something that gave me pleasure for 30 years and more. Willie had come to offer me two of his paintings, one of Tillysburn and the other of a point-to-point race, at a price of £5 each. To his great surprise – he told me I would never make a businessman – I paid him £50 for the pair, and I knew that even then I was getting a bargain. The paintings, which must now be worth a small fortune, were the first acquisitions of the Ulster Television Art Collection, which went on to become one of the finest of its kind in Northern Ireland. Our Board, of course, was reluctant but with the invaluable support of Lady Antrim I extracted a grudging consent to the project. In the years that followed I toured the Belfast galleries and openings, picking up the occasional bargain and gradually building the collection. My rules were that the artist had to be from Northern Ireland (although occasionally we dipped across the border) and that the pictures should be on display in Havelock House. Lady Antrim suggested one early purchase, a work by the itinerant artist Camille Souter, and we received an important boost when a private collector offered me the chance to buy several more Conors, including his scene at the Cenotaph and another of a Harland and Wolff launch. Theo Snoddy, an art historian and an old friend from *News Letter* days, catalogued the collection and it went on tour many times, serving as a wonderful flag carrier for the company in different parts of Northern Ireland.

This was not the limit of the company's support for the arts, for we did a lot of good work in the field of drama. We could not produce many plays on screen - our resources were too small and I refused to make anything that would be obviously threadbare - but we were active sponsors of the Arts Theatre in Belfast and, when it opened in 1965, of the Lyric. We also backed a body called the Ulster Centre for Theatre, Entertainment, Music and the Arts, whose mission was self-explanatory and whose chairman was Sir Tyrone Guthrie. He did not have the time to contribute much, but the centre's secretary, Michael Emmerson, went on to make a mark as the founding organizer of the Belfast Festival, another cause UTV helped to start. I will mention just one more because it is close to my heart, the Ulster Association of Drama Festivals, with which I retain a strong connection to this day and to which I will return later in this book. I must admit that all of this, though it allowed me to indulge my personal interests while winning friends for Ulster Television, was not entirely philanthropic in motivation - the Board might never have swallowed it if they had become aware. For one thing the Ulster drama world was a source of talent for us, providing most of our presenters, and for another, from 1963 onwards the ITA made grants to the arts and sciences mandatory for the companies, leaving no doubt that any company which failed would be in trouble when its contract came up for renewal. The expenditure duly appeared in our balance sheet and we once received a visit from a tax inspector who suggested that far from being 'necessary and proper expenditure' under the terms of the commercial tax laws, this was a taxable indulgence. When I explained that if we failed to make these payments we would be out of business he changed his tune.

In 1963 I took on an important responsibility outside Ulster Television when I became a member of the committee on higher education in Northern Ireland, chaired by Sir John Lockwood. One of the recommendations eventually made by this body became extremely controversial and the committee's work as a whole is widely misunderstood today, so I will take a moment to describe, from the inside, what really happened. The committee had four English members: Lockwood, who was Master of Birkbeck College, London; Lord Willis Jackson of Imperial College, London; Sir Peter Venables, Chancellor of the University of Aston and Dame Rosemary Murray, later Vice-Chancellor of Cambridge University. With them sat four members from Northern Ireland: Denis Rebbeck, chairman of Harland and Wolff; Willie Mol, headmaster of Ballymena Academy; Major John Glen, formerly of the Department of Education in Belfast, and me. It may have been my role in pioneering adult educational television with *Midnight Oil* which made me appear suitable for the task. I was persuaded to accept the assignment by David Holden of the Ministry of Finance, who told me, in a fine example of economy with the truth, that it would involve only one meeting of a few hours each month and the job would be 'over in a year'. Of course it was not so simple as that: the pile of documents we had to read eventually grew taller than myself, and I soon lost count of the number of meetings we held.

Student numbers were growing rapidly in Northern Ireland and estimates suggested that a total of 15,000 university places would be required by the end of the century. Even if this figure had been correct – and it proved a considerable underestimate – this was felt to be more than Queen's in Belfast could or should accommodate alone. There was an obvious need for a new institution and in fact we recommended two: the Ulster Polytechnic, which was established at

Newtownabbey, and the New University of Ulster, which was intended as a friendly rival and alternative to Queen's. It is chiefly for our recommendation on the location of the New University that the Lockwood Committee is remembered. There was general agreement that it should be sited outside Belfast and the locations proposed were Armagh, Coleraine, Craigavon and Derry. We felt that Craigavon was too close to Belfast, and also in too early a stage of its development to become home for a student body. Of the rest Derry, as Northern Ireland's second city, had the strongest claim and the committee went there to hear its case. The obvious nucleus for a university there would be Magee College, a curious institution which was established for the education of Presbyterian ministers but had since become part of the University of Dublin, while the city authorities had also earmarked a separate patch of land for the expansion which would be necessary. It was obvious that, unusually, the whole city was largely united in supporting this bid, and yet the committee members left the Maiden City with a feeling of unease.

Both groups, the English members and those, like myself, from the region, saw the creation of a new university as a significant departure for Northern Ireland and point the way to the future. This was about what should be done for and with the bright young Ulster people of the coming generations and we felt it important to help them escape from the past. Even before we went to Derry, therefore, we favoured a site that would give the new institution a fresh start with no baggage and no preconceptions. There were practical difficulties with the city's bid, such as the anomalous status of Magee and the awkwardness of a divided site, but there was also the problem of local politics, for it was obvious to all of us – and again this included the English members – that the apparent unity did not run deep. It was and had long been a bitterly divided city and the tensions which would soon make it world famous were there to be felt. It was for these reasons that the committee was uncomfortable with the Derry option, and some of the same factors applied to historic Armagh. Coleraine thus came to the fore and its bid had much to recommend it. The triangle of

Portrush, Portstewart and Coleraine offered a green-field site in both the physical and the historical sense. As a holiday area it was familiar to most Northern Ireland people and it had the advantage of offering plentiful off-season accommodation. The Coleraine sponsoring committee was made up of a diverse cross-section of local people with business, educational and cultural interests and there were opportunities to achieve excellence in academic fields which we felt Queen's could not offer, notably future aspects of agriculture and the maritime and environmental sciences.

This was no easy decision; it was tough and complex. The committee explored the issues conscientiously for a year and a half and the final debate was long, with Derry's sincere and passionate claims thoroughly and thoughtfully considered. What tipped the balance was the feeling that I have described: we wanted to draw students away from the past rather than place them in its midst. This gave the verdict to Coleraine. We had no idea then of the impact our proposal would have once it became government policy. In the emotional outburst that followed all our – as we thought – rational arguments – academic, sociological and financial – were drowned. Sir John Lockwood, for one, was a passionate advocate of integrated education and it was his careful diplomacy, including a private meeting with Cardinal Conway which I engineered, which paved the way for non-denominational teacher training. This has been forgotten. We chose Coleraine over Derry not because we were locked in the past but because we wanted the young people of Northern Ireland to escape from it.

My connection with higher education in Northern Ireland did not end there for I soon joined the governing bodies of both the New University and the Polytechnic and witnessed at first hand the tremendous work done by both institutions. Many years later the New University kindly gave me an honorary doctorate. I have never felt, however, that the place had the luck it deserved. The buildings were misconceived – I will never forget my horror when the charming centre of intellectual and social activity I had visualized for the banks of the Bann turned out to be a couple of tower blocks on a bleak, windswept hilltop. And there were also academic setbacks, such as the refusal of Queen's to accept our recommendation that its agriculture department should be transferred to Coleraine. As happened in ITV, the institution was frequently destabilized by official inquiries which tended to uproot the plant in the effort to establish how well it was growing. Today the Polytechnic and New University are one institution – the University of Ulster – and Northern Ireland has some 30,000 undergraduates at four sites: Belfast, Coleraine, Jordanstown and Derry.

I had another taste of the problems of academic life much later, when I was appointed the Crown representative on the Senate of Queen's University. There I watched as my brilliant friend from Trinity days, the Vice-Chancellor Peter Froggatt, played this unwieldy body of 70 members as if it were his personal violin. I contributed in various ways but I suspect that I was most useful in employment matters, which came to the Senate only when they reached crisis point. Few of my fellow-members had experience in this field, where the law is extremely arcane, unbalanced and vulnerable to abuse. For all their supposed unworldliness academics can be adept at playing these games, but having crossed swords so many times with the best negotiators the broadcasting unions could find, I think I had seen most of their tricks before.

9
The Great, the Good and the Others

London was where the power lay in Independent Television, where policies were made, strategic decisions taken and deals done. As a regional company Ulster Television always risked being forgotten so it was vital to make our voice heard at the centre, and that was my job. As a result I had the privilege of a grandstand seat for the most dramatic and most colourful days of commercial television. The people who founded the companies and the original leaders of the ITA were no grey television career-men because the medium had not been around long enough for that species to evolve. Instead they had brought with them experience - often distinguished experience - of other walks of life. In the case of the company men they tended to be adventurers, many of them self-made, with all the confidence and initiative that implied. A few were showmen, too. Their spirit saw ITV through its rocky early years and their style captured the audience and built the enormous success of later years.

None is more famous or perhaps notorious than Lew Grade, later Lord Lew. Though his name will always be linked with Associated Television (ATV) he was not, in fact, that company's founding genius - that was Norman Collins - and nor was he its first boss - that was Val Parnell. Both of those men deserve a word before I speak of Lew. Norman Collins was the bravest pioneer of ITV, a former BBC executive who early on envisaged the need and potential for commercial television in Britain and lobbied tirelessly and selflessly until it became a reality. At the launch of ATV he was deputy chairman but what power he had was washed away in the early financial storms and though he made his pile (and went on to become an adviser to the Conservative Party) I have always felt that he deserved better from the industry. Val Parnell, best known for his billing as executive producer of *Sunday Night at the*

London Palladium, was managing director when I had my first dealings with ATV, with Lew, a former Charleston dance champion who became a theatrical agent and impresario, as his deputy. By an unusual diktat of the ATV Board these two were forced to share an office – perhaps the directors thought they would keep each other out of trouble – but they salvaged privacy and dignity by taking a room as big as a tennis court and operating at opposite ends. Val liked to keep Lew in his place and I remember that at industry meetings he always positioned Lew behind him rather than beside him at the table. At regular intervals, while Lew was sending up clouds from his famous cigars, Val would produce a small Woodbine from a gold case and ostentatiously lean back to demand that his deputy furnish him with a light. Since I liked Val more than I did Lew I found this performance delightful.

But nothing could keep Lew Grade down for long and after Val's early death he was the power at the ATV. A shameless populist who believed in giving people what they wanted, he was a perfect fit for commercial television. Among his many famous lines was one uttered after watching a television play he didn't like: 'That must be culture because it sure ain't entertainment.' We often attended meetings together but my personal dealings with him in the 1960s were mostly to do with his 'mid-Atlantic' series, *The Baron*, *The Saint* and *The Prisoner*. These ambitious projects required financing, preferably up front from Lew's point of view, and for this he turned to the regional companies among others. I was chosen to negotiate with him and he would sometimes summon me to his office 'as early as you can my boy'. He always claimed he was at his desk by 6 a.m. every morning but I was never quite sure, so on one occasion I decided to call his bluff. Arriving at 8 a.m. I was gratified to find his secretary a little put out and, after making me comfortable, she vanished. It was half an hour later when a flustered Lew emerged from his inner sanctum muttering vaguely that he had 'been on the phone to the United States'. This was probably meant to impress me, but since it would have meant that somebody in New York was working at 3 a.m. I did not believe him and, with a furrowed brow and a glance at my watch, I made my scepticism obvious. It gave our subsequent negotiation a certain edge which did my side no harm at all.

He was impulsive, veering between generosity and toughness, and I found there were two tricks to doing business with him. One was to allow him to be as paternal (or patronising) as he liked – I always accepted the eight-inch cigars he handed out, as well as the homely advice and the insincere compliments – and the other, an old one, was always to say a firm 'no' to his first price. He liked to haggle and respected a tough negotiator, in fact I believe he enjoyed the trading more than the luxuries it brought him, even though the cigars and the Rolls-Royces with 'LG' number plates might suggest otherwise. Lew's great joy was the complicated transatlantic deal involving horse-trading between a dozen different parties with himself at the centre, the only one who could see the whole picture. This was how *The Saint* and the others came about. While he chose to involve the regional stations partly to balance the influence of the other leading ITV companies it was useful to us to pick up some chips in the big game, and from my personal point of view it was refreshing to be a buyer rather than a seller, since so much of my time in London was spent trying to convince sceptical metropolitans of the wonders of Ulster Television and the Northern Ireland market.

Lew's cigars have entered legend. He either smoked or gave away at least twenty of these torpedo-like objects a day and since they cost something like £5 each the annual bill must have been of the order of £20,000 – an astronomic sum even for ATV. And they could land him and others in trouble. I once attended a meeting at ATV house at a time when a big labour dispute was looming between the companies and the Association of Cine and Television Technicians. Hard work had been done before we met and the meeting was planned as a formality. Everything passed off smoothly, with handshakes exchanged, until Lew leapt up from behind Val to seal the agreement by handing out cigars. All present then set about the business of lighting them and though a few tentative puffs soon reached the air some around the table had a struggle. This pause, no part of the plan, gave time for eyes once again to fall upon the agreement and sure enough mischief followed. One of the union men asked: 'You see this clause ten? Could we make a couple of small changes there because I think some of the members won't be too happy?' Similar queries followed and before long, thanks to those infernal cigars, the whole gathering descended into open haggling which took several hours to resolve.

Tom Brownrigg was as different a character to Lew Grade as nature could have contrived. A former captain in the Royal Navy, he had served in Churchill's war rooms in Whitehall and when peace came reorganized the dockyards in Singapore. Like many naval men he was a stickler in all things, sometimes to the point of absurdity. He once sent two memos to a drama director at the same time, one to congratulate him on a play broadcast the previous evening and the other to inform him he was being made redundant because of an economy drive. He saw nothing odd about this: each was 'the right thing to do' and the coincidence, though unfortunate, made not the smallest difference. Perhaps it was in his dress, however, that Tom's fastidiousness showed most starkly, for he was always immaculately turned out according to the strictest code. On one occasion, for example, he turned up for a meeting in a magnificent morning suit complete with tails and topper and explained without embarrassment that as soon as we finished he was off to Ascot for cocktails. On another he complimented me on my dark grey suit, observing that 'only bounders wear blue suits before 6 p.m.'. Directly behind me at that moment stood Lord Antrim, wearing just such a suit; I never knew whether he heard but relations between them were difficult anyway (partly because Tom insisted on referring to my chairman as Lord Ampthill). For years Tom called me simply 'Henderson' in his brisk quarterdeck manner, until the day it occurred to him I might be related to Oscar Henderson. When I confirmed that I was Oscar's son he was delighted, explaining that he had once served under my father (whom he described with approval as 'a terror') in the Far East. From then on it was 'Tom' and 'Brum' and we were warm friends.

None of this eccentricity prevented Tom Brownrigg from being an exemplary general manager at Associated-Rediffusion. Though a talkative man he was efficient and wise and he always did his homework – it was no accident that he was the person who thrashed out that deal with George Elvin. His naval ways, which permeated A-R, had the knack of making sure things got done and they influenced my own management style for many years. It was Tom who introduced me to the 'action column', a device which ensured, as he put it, that 'people did not sit on their bums between meetings'. He also believed in regular management gatherings first thing on Monday and last thing on Friday, with never more than two drinks served at the latter. My favourite memory of Tom at work relates to the Independent Television Companies Association where he chaired a committee of three set up with the intention of making the association more useful than it had been. I was one of them and when I arrived at the key meeting I found 40 pages of foolscap before me, painstakingly prepared and logically presented by Brownrigg himself. All we had to do was run though this fine document, which did not take long, and when we reached the end the chairman snapped shut his file with satisfaction and announced: 'Cocktail time!' That plan went through unaltered and guided the association's workings for many years.

Associated-Rediffusion, which served the London area, was for practical purposes a subsidiary of British Electric Traction, the conglomerate built up by Harley Drayton. It had begun as a joint venture with Associated Newspapers, the owners of the *Daily Mail*, but they sold up when the going got tough and BET carried on alone. A-R had an admirably small Board of just five members, who did not include Brownrigg because there was also a Managing Director, Paul Adorian, about whom I should say a few words. Adorian was one of those who mortgaged his home in the troubled early years to keep the business going, and one of his lasting marks on ITV was to foster its interest in sport, from tennis (which he loved) to horse racing and swimming. An Armenian by origin and an electrical engineer of distinction by background, he lent further variety and experience to our little world, and he also took an interest in me. One of BET's many properties was Wembley Stadium and one day, when Northern Ireland were playing England, he invited me to watch in the directors' box and lavished a surprising amount of attention on me. A little later I found myself his guest again, this time at the Athenaeum and in the presence of the A-R Chairman, John Wills. It turned out that they were courting me and I was offered a senior position at BET, although not initially on the television side because 'we will have to shift a few people'. This was a glittering offer, with more money, a house in London and prospects in one of the biggest companies around, and as Paul drove me to the airport for my flight to Belfast he gave a strong impression that I would be mad to turn it down. But when I got home doubts crept in: my marriage was still limping to its end and my father was ill, so the timing was bad. I also liked my life at Ulster Television and I wasn't sure I wanted another job. And one small thing about that Athenaeum lunch nagged at me: each time John Wills emptied his wine glass, I had noticed, he didn't pour himself a fresh one but indicated by a look to Paul that he was ready for a top-up. This seemed a regal way for a businessman to behave and it made me wonder about my future role with them. In the end I declined the offer and Paul, always a gentleman, never held it against me.

Granada had the weekday contract to broadcast in the north of England and was the domain of the remarkable Bernstein brothers, owners of a large chain of cinemas. A canny pair, they joked that they chose Manchester as their headquarters because the north-west was the country's wettest region and people had little choice but to stay in and watch television. This proved to contain more than a grain of truth because Granada developed a peculiar problem which it shared with Ulster Television: so loyal were the viewers in our two rainy regions that advertisers found they could reach their whole potential market with just a handful of advertisements, whereas elsewhere they needed more to drive the same message home. Our success in attracting viewers, in other words, was counting against us in advertising sales. (I once tried to 'damp down' the audience by placing a discussion programme in the middle of Wednesday evening, only to find the ratings improving and the ITA patting me on the back for my commitment to serious programming.) Of the two Bernsteins Sydney was the outgoing one, an entrepreneur with great style and flair, while Cecil was more thoughtful. Cecil's was the fertile brain that gave us *The Army Game, All Our Yesterdays, World in Action* and above all *Coronation Street*. Like Lew Grade he usually travelled in a big car and legend has it that he once tried to ring Lew when Lew was in his Rolls, only to be told by the chauffeur that 'the boss is on the other line'. Under the Bernsteins Granada was always a company with style and originality but also with a good, reliable, popular touch.

Granada did not have a Programme Controller by name but the man who carried out that role was another important figure, Denis Forman. He had come from the film industry and went on to be Chairman of Granada Television and a knight of the realm, but in these early days he was very senior in the company. Once when I was in his office the phone rang and he answered, immediately rising to his feet and answering 'Yes, Mr Sydney' to a flood of instructions. Although most of us in the industry, despite Tom Brownrigg's views, tended to wear blue suits, Denis always wore grey flannel and he had a good explanation. His father had been a Presbyterian minister and a generous tailor in the congregation gave him a bolt of clerical grey flannel every Christmas. When Forman *pere* died, Forman *fils* inherited the accumulated stock and was far too thrifty not to use it. He was a big man too and as we stood together once I asked him what he weighed. 'Twelve stone,' he replied. 'Nonsense,' I exclaimed. But he tapped his leg and said: 'Monte Cassino.' It was false, and aluminium is a lot lighter than flesh and bone.

Last of the Big Four companies of the 1960s was ABC, the outfit we at Ulster Television knew best. ABC had the contract for weekend broadcasts in the North and Midlands, an odd arrangement and a consolation prize of sorts for the Associated British Picture Corporation (owned by Warner Brothers of Hollywood), which had wanted a bigger slice of commercial television. Again the Board was small and it included two men we have already met:

Howard Thomas and George Cooper. Howard was a highly creative manager with a good eye for talent who, before ABC, had worked in radio and at Pathe news, but George was a character of a different kind. Austere rather than flamboyant, he was none the less a fine salesman who had that special characteristic of the breed: he never let a chance go by. My favourite example of this was at Cannes. One of the perks of our trade was the annual international advertising trade conference, usually held in the Riviera resort. Many commercials were viewed (I once saw 1,400 in a week), many large meals eaten and many bottles emptied, and along the way most of the delegates found a little time for the beach. One day George was sunbathing after a dip in the Med when a passing advertiser spotted him and inquired about the price of a commercial on ABC, giving precise details: thirty seconds, Midlands only, Saturday evening etc. 'Just a ball-park figure of course,' said the advertiser, but the ever-ready George could do better than that. Unzipping a pocket in his still-wet trunks, he extracted an ABC rate card – laminated, of course – and quoted the exact price. He had a deservedly long career in ITV, first succeeding Howard as managing director at Thames Television and later becoming chairman of *TV Times*.

ATV, Associated-Rediffusion, Granada and ABC: together these were the heart of the network for most of the sixties. Rich in original personalities and full of ambition and talent, they had their alliances and rivalries, their jealousies and foibles. The job of keeping them in order, along with the smaller regional companies such as Scottish, Southern, Tyne Tees and Ulster, fell to the Independent Television Authority. This was the usual worthy body, with a distinguished Chairman, a board of notable members, a Director General and a secretariat, all of them lodged in prestigious London premises, first in the former American embassy at Princes Gate and later opposite Harrods in Brompton Road. Of all these people it was the Director General – the 'D.G.' – who got things done and from the birth of commercial television until the early seventies that post was held by the great Sir Robert Fraser. A one-time journalist knighted for his work at the Central Office of Information, Fraser was a smooth man full of brains and charm who had done as much as anyone to hold ITV together in the days when it looked as though the companies might go bust. For us on the company side he was the key figure not least because he chaired the Standing Consultative Committee at which most of the collective business with the companies was done. As is often the case with people practised in the Whitehall arts Fraser's management style was subtle to the point of guile. When things became too delicate to be handled in committee he would invite a managing director for a walk in the park during which he would fish artfully for information and opinions while himself letting drop the odd calculated indiscretion; both sides tended to benefit.

My own dealings with him were friendly, though formal. He showed understanding towards Ulster Television in our earliest years, giving us time and leeway to find our feet, and in the mid-60s I once again had cause to seek his indulgence. The first surge of success and profits had passed and we were once again conscious of the burden of the large annual rental we paid to the ITA. A variety of factors made this seem unfair, not least that problem we shared with Granada of being too successful at delivering audiences to our advertisers, and it was decided that I should raise this with the Authority. Taking a leaf from Fraser's own book I wanted to broach this outside the ITA offices so I invited him to lunch at the White House, which was close to our London sales office and a favourite venue for entertaining advertisers. It did not go to plan. We were greeted and seated by Leno, the flamboyant *maitre d'*, who of course knew me very well. When Sir Robert asked for a small pale sherry Leno, without a pause, replied: 'Certainly sir. And for you Mr 'enderson, the usual large Scotch?' I nodded, glancing uneasily at my guest. Immune to hints and winks, Leno addressed Fraser again: 'To begin, can I offer some asparagus we 'ave specially flown in this morning from California?' The DG ordered consommé. 'After that, per'aps some of our specially prepared pheasant?' No thank you, he would have cold beef with green salad. 'And for you, Mr 'enderson, the asparagus of course, and your usual pressed duck?' Wincing, I nodded again and hoped it was over, but no. As he turned away, Leno delivered the final blow: 'And of course the magnum of the Marbuset.' I don't like to think what impression this gave of me personally to the frugal Sir Robert, who eventually accepted just half a glass of our top-notch claret, but I knew that it hardly suggested – as I was about to argue – that Ulster Television was on its uppers. For the next hour I sweated through a very awkward lunch and the DG probably relished every moment of my embarrassment, though he was gracious enough at the end to acknowledge merit in the argument that the rental was unfair. Alas, he said, there was little he could do.

That White House lunch is a story with several morals. The first is that when inviting an important personage to lunch take due account of his or her tastes. The second is when going to a place where you are known it is wise to brief the staff in advance. The third, perhaps, is that good arguments do not always carry the day. Whatever the surroundings, my plea of hardship at that lunch was not false and we and other companies endured a couple of lean years in the 60s – at Ulster Television we even cancelled the dividend on one occasion. As for the pressed duck and Marbuset I make no apologies: no matter how hard-up we were, and irrespective of whether we enjoyed it or not, television executives were required to please advertisers. That was the rule and I liked it that way.

Fraser worked for a succession of very different ITA Chairmen. I had come along too late to have dealings with the first, who was the art historian Kenneth Clark, (and father of the late diarist and MP Alan Clark). The second Chairman, Sir Ivone Kirkpatrick, I met just twice. A retired Foreign Office mandarin, his principal claim to fame was that it was he who greeted Rudolf Hess upon his unexpected arrival in Britain during the war. The first of my encounters with Sir Ivone was on Ulster Television's launch day in 1958 and I confess I have little memory of it. The second took place in London a couple of years later as we both left a dreadful party thrown to mark the ITA's move to Brompton Road. As we rode down in the lift I broke a long, polite silence by observing: 'Very nice party, thank you, sir.' To this he replied simply: 'Yes.' Another awkward pause ensued until the doors opened and he strode away with the words: 'Goodnight Henderson ... and good luck.' It worried me for weeks.

By contrast the third Chairman, Charles Hill, Lord Hill of Luton, I came to know well, both for good and ill. A busy man who smoked a pipe in the manner of Popeye, he walked with short, quick strides that suggested an urgent need to set about sinners, which was precisely what he thought he was doing at Independent Television. Not long after his appointment we had gathered at the ITA offices for a meeting of the Standing Consultative Committee with Fraser in charge. After this ended Fraser asked us to stay in our places for the first session of a new body called the Programme Policy Committee which, he added laconically, 'our new chairman sees himself chairing'. With that he slid his slender frame sideways from the chairman's seat as, seemingly on cue, Hill bustled into the room. Plonking himself down at the head of the table and placing his pipe in an ashtray, he declared: 'Gentlemen, the programmes – in the view of the Authority – are pretty bloody.'

Hill was like a character from Tudor England, blunt, clever and intimidating but also capable of kindness and vulnerability. He had won national fame on the BBC as the 'Radio Doctor' who was so keen for us to keep our bowels moving, and then served as Postmaster General – in which capacity he had observed closely the birth of commercial television. He did not like the way that our affairs had developed and came to the ITA on a mission, whether of his own design or the government's we never knew, to 'sort that lot out'. Hill was deeply suspicious of cosiness and complacency and he plainly detected both in ITV, besides which there were some ITV programmes which he hated with a passion. To us a hands-on Chairman was as unwelcome as it was unfamiliar, but we were in for a shake-up and we had no choice in the matter. One of his hates was the wrestling. 'It is a fraud and it should continue no longer,' he told us. 'Can any of you gentlemen give me one good reason why it should not cease?' Of course there was a very good reason, which was that it was extremely popular, particularly among housewives and, therefore, advertisers. But Hill did not want to hear that; what concerned him was that it was staged, that the fights were not real fights. He fixed his eye on Lew: 'I notice, Mr Grade, that you are uncharacteristically silent. Do you wish to defend this deception perpetrated upon the British public?' Lew replied: 'My lord, I always say if you can't fake it, it ain't real.' The wrestling disappeared. Another of his pet hates was quiz games and he waged a long campaign against them, with mixed results. And yet another was the much-loved and shambolic *Crossroads*, but although Hill frequently complained about it and managed to cut its weekly showings, Meg, Jill, Sandy and Amy Turtle were still there when he left us.

Hill brought a new disease to Independent Television: navel contemplation. Under his gimlet eye we were subjected to a dreary round of conferences, conventions, seminars and symposia, the purpose of which, I suspect, was to infuse us with some sense of common purpose and culture. Inevitably the result was to infuse us either with alcohol or with a burning desire to be elsewhere and I cannot recall learning anything of use. Hill was interested in centralizing, in giving London more control over what had been a vigorous federal system, and one of the ways he found of doing this was to replace our various programme guides with a national *TV Times*. Publicly he always said this initiative was meant to improve our image by giving us a sleek and glossy magazine, but few of us accepted this logic. When the news was broken I remember Lew leaping to the defence of his own guide, *TV World*, and being told that it was 'quite ghastly'. He continued to protest until Fraser, fixing him with a cold look, said: 'Oh come off it, Lew.' For us in Belfast the change was also unwelcome since our *TV Post*, for all that it was monochrome and printed on plain newsprint, had won a large readership which *TV Times* would never match, even many years later when Northern Ireland had twice as many television sets as it did in the 1960s.

The ultimate weapon in the ITA's hands, if a company displeased it, was dismissal. Every few years the licences came up for renewal and the Authority could require each company to justify its record and its right to another contract. If alternative bidders came along there would be a contest, or if the ITA chose to meddle with things it could do so. In 1967-68, under Hill, it meddled in a big way. The big four all found their licences altered for the worse, a couple of them dramatically, while two big new companies were created: Yorkshire and London Weekend. ABC became a new company – Thames Television. When the dust settled there were five big companies instead of four: Granada, ATV, Thames, Yorkshire and London Weekend, and although the rearrangement left all the stations outside the London area operating over the full seven days, I never saw it as a gain. Yorkshire in particular was a misjudgement. The new area's advertising potential was relatively small, below that of Southern Television and near Anglia's, and yet it was supposed to be a big player in the network.

Happily Ulster Television survived unchanged, although not without enduring some unpleasantness. No other bid was mounted for the Northern Ireland contract but Hill insisted that we appear to make our case. Our team consisted of Lord Antrim, William MacQuitty, Sir Francis Evans, Mike Hutcheson, Barry Johnston and myself and I knew before it began that it would be a sticky business, not least because Hill was another man who did not get on with our Chairman – he had once stayed as a guest at Lord Antrim's home, Glenarm Castle, and the mood had been frosty to say the least.

It was an uneasy party who marched in to face the inquisition and we made a poor fist of our presentation. Sharp questions followed, to which we gave poor answers and I felt trouble brewing. Although we had resolved to be pragmatic and low-key – having learned the lesson of our grand promises in 1958 – I suddenly decided we had nothing to lose and launched into a peroration about our ambitions. These were still early days for us, I said, and we were still adjusting, but in the course of the next contract I could see us developing many splendid new ideas and programmes and delivering all the rest of our original promises. My colleagues were aghast at this unauthorized outburst but it seemed to do some good – it could hardly have made things worse. We survived the grilling and, if only because there was no alternative, we kept our contract.

10
Troubled Times

From the vantage point of the 21st century it can be difficult to see the 1960s in Northern Ireland as anything more than a prelude to the Troubles. Thirty years of violence lay ahead; surely it must have been obvious that those divisions would burst to the surface? Well, perhaps it should have been, but I doubt if anyone around in those years, Protestant or Catholic, foresaw with any accuracy what would happen. We knew that there were problems and tensions but by and large they seemed to be old ones, at least as old as Northern Ireland itself, which by then had existed for some 40 years and had survived successive IRA campaigns without difficulty. We knew that there would have to be changes but there was little to suggest that the place was a pressure cooker whose lid was about to blow off. In hindsight this may seem surprising but it was not a view held only by locals, for visitors from outside tended to form the same impression – even such sceptics as Tim Hewat, one of the journalistic lions of Granada's *World in Action* programme. Hewat spent a week in Belfast scouting for programme ideas in the mid-60s, using Havelock House as his base, and departed without a story – he could not find anything in Northern Ireland interesting enough to capture the interest of the British public.

What I remember most from those years is a sense of *ennui* and a hunger for change and modernity. To the young – I was still in my 30s – the place seemed insular and fuddy-duddy. These were the Swinging Sixties elsewhere, but while our economy was slowly being modernised much of Northern Ireland life was lagging behind. It wasn't just a matter of disputes over padlocking playground swings on Sundays but of a more general straitjacket of old-fashioned attitudes. Ulster Television, I felt, brought in some fresh air. We were new, we were locally-based and we were hugely popular, while the ITV programmes we carried in those days, though they might seem tame today, were challenging and ground-breaking in their time. Through us, Ulster people could gain a wider view of the modern world, or so we, somewhat arrogantly, believed.

Local politics of the conventional kind were largely stale and quiet, so that even after our news service began operating they caused us few difficulties – in fact we never had a dispute over news coverage with the Stormont government before 1968. No doubt this reflected the Unionist establishment's fundamental lack of interest in 'public relations' – Lord Brookeborough, the Prime Minister from 1943 to 1963, seemed to behave as though broadcasting did not exist but his successor, Terence O'Neill, took more interest. O'Neill was no screen performer. True, with his patrician manner and Etonian accent, he was never going to be clasped to the bosoms of the Shankill and the Falls but he was a man of integrity and could have won many more hearts and minds if he had been able to project himself. He was interviewed on *Newsview* and its successor, *UTV Reports*, and his hooded eyes, though a blameless physical characteristic, suggested shiftiness or arrogance. When I hinted politely that he might overcome this by pitching his gaze above the camera or above the interviewer's head he could – or would – not see the point but, much later, Willie Whitelaw did. These two pivotal figures had the same physical television handicap.

The political figure who inevitably caused some difficulty was Dr Ian Paisley. Though his following in the mid-60s was still small, he saw television as one means of changing this and of course we could not be exploited. He and I had already clashed in my *News Letter* days when he came to complain about a report and I was the lucky person delegated to deal with him. He has a remarkable memory so no doubt recalled this encounter when our paths crossed again. He was ambitious: he wanted to be a politician and to appear on news programmes to air his political views but at the same time he was also determined to be a clergyman and speak in religious programmes. On one occasion, after we had broadcast an interview with the ecumenical figure George Macleod of Iona, Paisley appeared outside Havelock House in his trademark white raincoat to lead a protest demonstration. It was not an impressive event since it consisted of just three people besides himself and by then we had experience of proper crowds, having coped for example with a large mob of people at the door desperate for a sight of the visiting Bruce Forsyth (I smuggled him out the back way) – and this was the route for other notables including Hughie Green, Gerry Fitt and Paddy Devlin.

There were other hard-line unionists with seats in Stormont or even Westminster and, since they spoke for more than themselves, they could demand air time. By the same token we broadcast the views of prominent nationalists, both those of the old school, such as Eddie McAteer, and the rising younger figures such as Gerry Fitt and John Hume. (Incidentally, McAteer came to me once to complain bitterly that we were giving Hume too much air time.) As far as was possible our news reports and discussion programmes embraced the full range of representative opinion, Green and Orange and Left and Right. Although this may sound like company policy it was more pragmatic than that: my responsibility was to encourage the newsmen get on with their job. And to back them. The Board neither knew nor cared about such matters and certainly they never tried to influence me or the news staff on any political coverage. We were therefore free and independent. Where I did have a policy was in the make-up of the newsroom itself. We hired good journalists with strong local track records and we never allowed one religion to dominate the team. Bill McGookin, Fred Corbett, Derek Murray, Rory Fitzpatrick, Paddy Scott, Robin Walsh, Ian Sanderson, Colm McWilliams and many others worked together to give us good, balanced news coverage reflecting all of Northern Ireland life. There was no question, then or later, of Ulster Television being a unionist or nationalist station in the way that the region's daily papers were. Senior colleagues, such as Jim Creagh and Brian Waddell, were significant figures in our question of 'balance'.

The ITA would never have permitted bias but this was not a matter of regulation. Nor, as some have suggested, was it driven by commercial motives - a fear of alienating one or other part of our advertising market. We were, for the most part, young people and we were in a new medium; our attitudes and practices were as modern and fair as we could manage. I could not have acted in any other way. Unlike my brother, who remained at the helm of the *News Letter*, I was not a member of the Unionist Party or of the Orange Order. Thanks largely to excessive compulsory worship at Bradfield I no longer even went to church and therefore could not be unjustly accused of bias. My politics were middle-of-the-road - akin, I suppose, to those later developed by the Alliance Party - and my Trinity past had helped me understand both the Red and the Green. So, although I was no firebrand reformer, I was no traditional Northern Ireland establishment figure either and I hope this was reflected in the staff, the programmes and the coverage.

As the outbreak of the Troubles approached, my personal life was in transition. In 1967, after years of woes and a failed reconciliation, Joy and I finally parted. After lonely and unhappy months I was lucky enough to meet and fall in love with Patricia Davison. She worked at Ulster Television as P.A. to a senior colleague and I had noticed her about the office and spoken to her several times before I plucked up the courage to invite her out. Soon it was a romance, although a discreet one, since this was an office relationship and we were both shy of gossip. Then Pat took a job in London and we were able to conduct our courtship with more privacy. Resolved on marriage, I introduced her to my parents and this led to a curious little scene of which I heard nothing until years later. My father took Pat to another room and told her that, like many of the men in my family, I was a drinker. She should beware of this, he said, because it could lead to trouble. Pat kept this story to herself until long after our wedding and I am glad of it. I am sure that my father acted out of kindness for that was his way, but it seemed a strange thing to do.

We loved each other deeply, my father and I, and it was a great blow when he died in 1969. He had been a war hero. In the thick of the battle at Zeebrugge in 1918 he took charge of a converted Mersey ferry which was to land a force of Marines on the harbour 'mole' or pier.

His vessel bore the brunt of German shelling, suffering terrible casualties, but he successfully extricated it from the fighting, saving 10 lives out of the gallant 120 who had embarked. It was for this that he was awarded the D.S.O.. In my mother, who was known as Molly, he had married a genuine beauty of the time and theirs was a long and essentially happy union. Although they argued at times - often over money, or what she perceived as the shortage of it - he adored her. As a father he was undemonstrative and usually distant, which was the style in that age and class, but he was also fair and wise. Where Bill was the apple of my mother's eye I might have been my father's favourite. (Something of this could be seen, perhaps, in the sports and games which dominated our family life, for whether we played golf, tennis or cards Bill was my mother's partner while I was my father's.) It was especially poignant that it was my father who first had the vision of a local independent television channel, the vision which I helped make a reality. I know he was sad to leave the Board of Ulster Television, but equally I know that he was proud of my role in the company. He was more broad-minded than men of his background are supposed to have been, and having worked so loyally all those years at Government House he was devoted to Northern Ireland. Not long after his death Lily Smith, the much-loved family cook for five decades, would make a remark that for all its comic perversity contained a core of truth. 'It's a good job the Commander died when he did,' she declared, 'for if he hadn't, the Troubles would have killed him.'

Saturday 5th October 1968 is, in my view, the real date on which those Troubles began. Of course the preceding weeks and months had seen harbingers - in Caledon, Coalisland and Dungannon. All of these had been reported on Ulster Television, but it was that afternoon in Derry, or Londonderry, or the Maiden City which broke the old Northern Ireland asunder. And it was television, the new mass medium, which played the crucial part, the vivid pictures of policemen batoning demonstrators creating an international sensation. After the heady events that year in Prague, Paris and the United States,

Northern Ireland was suddenly a focus of world concern. Most significantly, British public opinion was dramatically stirred.

From that moment our world changed. The company which I had called a 'fun factory', the purveyor of popular entertainment to the people of Ulster, swiftly became a current affairs machine. Broadcasters accustomed to an environment of boring stability, where political change was glacial in pace and violent crime rare, found themselves in a fast-moving, brutal and almost bewildering political vortex and they tried their best to communicate what was happening to their audience. More than that, ethical questions which had previously seemed arcane became the stuff of urgent daily discussions and decisions. It was not new for us alone; it was new in a worldwide sense. Never before had journalists, editors and executives been placed in such a position. Here was a new medium with an unprecedented hook on people's emotions operating in a small and divided society which was in a state of the highest anxiety. Our coverage was breathtakingly swift by the standards of those years. People who were involved in an event in, say, Armagh or Ballymena in the afternoon could see it reported, with pictures, on *UTV Reports* at 6 p.m. More than that, they would see immediate reaction and comment, and later in the evening perhaps a studio discussion about the implications. Nothing like this – with all the immediacy and impact of fresh moving pictures – had occurred before. This was to place on broadcasters unexpected and heavy burdens.

I had a glimpse of what was to come on that very first day. Our cameraman at the Derry events was Ken Orbinson, who arrived there in good time and met the Civil Rights Association organizers of the march. They explained what they expected to happen and took him to a location where they said he would have a good view. They did not disappoint. As the events unfolded Orbinson was perfectly placed to record the clashes between police and protesters – so well-placed, in fact, that he was actually soaked by a police water cannon. When the worst was over he threw his camera in the back of his car and rushed off by road back to Belfast to present his film for editing and broadcast. It was as I listened to his account of

Surveying the Belfast skyline with James Prior (Secretary of State) in the 80s

Glynis and I greeting David Plowright (brother of actress Joan Plowright), Managing Director of Granada, at a Television Symposium in Manchester, 1981 (the gentleman behind seems somewhat disturbed!)

Presenting Mr and Mrs Peter Bowles to Her Majesty the Queen at the Royal Television Society's Diamond Jubilee banquet in London, 1987; Fred Wylie (Chairman of the Northern Ireland branch of the RTS) is to my left

Bryan Murray and Peter Bowles in *Irish R.M.* costume – a highly successful co-production with Channel 4

This amusing Natural Break cartoon appeared in the 1980s. The caption reads: 'I've heard of the tallest and heaviest but the youngest M.D. ...'

Ralph Dobson's topical cartoon montage of 1982, which graced the cover of the October edition of the *Trade and Industry Board Room Magazine*. It celebrated the mixed feelings in ITV about the arrival of Channel 4.

Co-operation Ireland – with Maureen O'Hara and Tommy Fegan (Deputy C.E.O.), early 1990s

Co-operation North golf in Edinburgh with Kevan Whitson (Royal Co. Down Professional) and Jimmy Hill

Speaking to the Rotary Club of Naples, Florida in the 1990s (part of many efforts to explain issues around Northern Ireland for Co-operation Ireland)

Farewell to Co-operation Ireland. Tony Kennedy (C.E.O.) presents the Bird of Peace with Vernon O'Byrne (Company Secretary), 1999

The first Board of Laganside with John Carson (former Lord Mayor of Belfast), George Mackey (C.E.O.), the Duke of Abercorn (Chairman) and Margaret Spence-Silcock, c.1990

Ulster Waterways – another propaganda effort to show their tourist potential

A group of past Presidents of the Northern Ireland Chamber of Commerce and Industry gather on the stairs of the Culloden Hotel, Holywood, Co. Down for the annual dinner, late 1990s

The Ballynahinch murals – one of the annual receptions, 2001. Left to right: Vincent Fullam (Chairman, Ballynahinch Regeneration Ltd), Jim Wells M.L.A., Councillor Albert Colmer, Anne McAleenan (Chairman, Down District Council), Eamon O'Neill M.L.A.

A little more time for golf – in front of the 1895 Royal Co. Down clubhouse, 2002

With the Captain of Royal Co. Down Terry Hutley (left) and Rick Neet, the Head Professional of Royal Palm, Naples, Florida, at the famous steps of the Royal Co. Down clubhouse

Pat holds William as a baby

Pat and Glynis at my 70th birthday party

Sally and William amuse Pat, 2001

Doctored again! – after the graduation ceremony at Queen's University, Belfast, with Chris Gibson (far left), Sir George Bain (Vice-Chancellor) and Brenda McLaughlin (Pro-Chancellor), Summer 2002

the day (he was eager to have his suit replaced at company expense) that the complexities of the situation dawned on me. I saw that we could be used by others to project the images which they wanted to see broadcast. It might be the police or the army, it might be loyalists or republicans, it might be politicians or rioters; we would have to be careful.

Just how careful was driven home to me soon, when rioting was commonplace, particularly in Belfast. One Saturday afternoon I was in the newsroom when a telephone rang next to me and I picked it up. 'Where are yer cameras?' asked a strongly-accented voice on the other end of the line. 'What cameras?' I replied, a little baffled. 'The cameras till cover the riot,' said the voice, with a hint of impatience. 'What riot? Where?' I asked, for our regular sources had no reports of trouble. 'Ye know fine well,' barked the caller, adding: 'The riot'll not start till yer cameras get here.' It is amusing in retrospect but it alarmed me at the time. We knew that demonstrations and so on were sometimes staged to attract coverage but that things had reached the point where people would ring up demanding cameras and then wait until they had arrived before starting their riot was the stuff of nightmares. We could cause violence rather than report it.

We learned quickly that news and comment could also inflame opinion. Nerves were raw and passions ran high; allegations and rumours ran like wildfire without any help from broadcasters, but television had unique power. Everybody, it seemed, was watching news bulletins and other programmes dealing with the Troubles, and everything we broadcast offended or outraged somebody, no matter how careful we were. Sometimes people were so angry about what they saw that blood was spilled. It was a heavy responsibility and I gradually learned that there was no comfortable, easy way of discharging it.

One constant pressure, especially once the IRA bombing campaign had begun, was concern about a direct attack on Ulster Television itself. An overriding worry was the threat to the life and limb of our now sizeable staff and I was not prepared to take foolish risks on that front. We often joked between ourselves that no one with any concern for public opinion would plant a bomb which would deny Northern Ireland its regular fixes of *Coronation Street* and *Crossroads*, but the danger was real, as was proved one night in the late 1970s when Havelock House was bombed. It was mid-evening when I got the call and I rushed there to find the staff out on the street but the building mercifully intact. More than a dozen firebombs had gone off around the outside walls, but while they caused scorching and blackening there was no serious damage; we had been saved by the wire fences protecting the windows. Programmes were off the air most of the night. Naturally we had made preparations for such attacks. We were determined to keep transmitting if at all possible – in the worst case I had arranged for us to operate from the studios of Border Television in Carlisle, with live programmes and commercials included. We also did what we could to automate transmission and this stood us in good stead on the many occasions when hoax calls or warnings forced us to evacuate the building temporarily. I took all of this not just seriously but personally: not only was it usually my task to decide whether to evacuate or not in the event of a threat, but the health and survival of the station were close to my heart. I was also the target of personal threats; my life was threatened some 40 times, most often in those early years. Sometimes the calls came through on my direct line in the office, telling me I was about to be shot for something we had broadcast or were about to broadcast or had decided not to broadcast. Sometimes they came on my unlisted number. In later years I pointed out to the callers (truthfully) that my insurance arrangements were such that my family would be much better off if I were dead. I usually reported the threats and the RUC offered me a gun for my protection which I declined. After a spate of calls, I looked out of my office window towards the old gasworks across the road and noticed that a slit had been cut in the brickwork crowning the roof. Peering across, I discerned the glint of a rifle barrel and I fancied that this was an army sniper stationed to watch over me. In the weeks that followed I could not resist pointing out my 'guardian angel' to people visiting my office. He soon moved on to more useful work.

Through all those early years of the Troubles our small team worked tirelessly to provide the best coverage we could. I have mentioned in particular Jim Creagh, who went on to become my deputy, Brian Waddell, later Programme Controller. Robin Walsh our News Editor was a hungry newsman, intensely determined, and I remember him pressing me constantly for additional men, equipment and air time to enable him to do justice to the dramas then unfolding. 'For God's sake, Brum...' was a sort of mantra in his conversation. I also remember long nights of poker dice with him and others as we tried to shake off the tensions of the day. On screen were the likes of David Mahlowe, Gordon Burns and Brian Baird, all of whom did distinguished work. Others in the backroom team were Geoffrey Gilbert, Sydney Perry and Tony Finigan, recruited from ABC, while our special heroes were the camera crews, of whom the best known were Sean McGaffin and Jim McGirr, known affectionately as Steptoe and Son. They had to endure life in the front line. Early in the Troubles we added an extra programme to our schedules with *Flashpoint*, a 30-minute nightly news programme at 10.30 p.m. intended to bring people up to date with the news and issues of the day. Produced by Derek Bailey, whom we re-hired from ATV, and presented mainly by Mahlowe and Derek Murray, it became the most intensely watched programme of its kind anywhere in British television as well as one of the most controversial. We had to tread a fine line: any hint, for example, that an interviewer had given a particular politician an easy ride, or had been unfair or over-hostile, could provoke outrage. Any report that presented disputed information as fact would bring a stream of protest.

The clergy, painstakingly cultivated in our earliest years, played an important part in our response to the violence. We had made valuable contacts through *End the Day* and various religious discussion programmes and we had an impressive advisory panel of clerics. More than that, we had excellent relations with the leaders of all four main churches, who appeared on a special programme before Christmas each year (and whom we always entertained to a good lunch). When the Troubles came we gladly gave air time to the soothing words of the clergy and they always rose impressively to the challenge. Father Hugh Murphy and Dr Jack Withers were notable successes, as were the Rev. David Burke and the young Rev. Robin Eames (later Church of Ireland Archbishop of Armagh), but I particularly remember the contribution one terrible night of Rev. Eric Gallagher. As riots raged across the city we sent a taxi for him and when he arrived hustled him straight into the 'announcer's box' to deliver his homily. Without a note he spoke for 17 minutes, offering viewers the soundest good sense and the finest Christian preaching they could have heard at such a time. When afterwards I congratulated him he thanked me for 'a valuable couple of minutes' and I had great delight in telling him he had had been rather longer than that on air, indeed probably long enough for an entry in the *Guinness Book of Records*.

Although it was never our policy to downplay the violence or the problems behind it we did our best to promote calm and dialogue. Equally, our programmes reflected the fact that, while the riots and bombings occupied the headlines, throughout most of Northern Ireland normal life went on as before. Despite being dominated by the big story, the news programmes found time to cover economic affairs, 'ordinary' crime, show business and matters of human interest. I will not list them, but in these years we also made a great variety of programmes unrelated to the Troubles in the realms of education, rural affairs, drama and light entertainment. We had more than one string to our bow and it should be no surprise that as the 1970s dawned we were no longer producing the one hour a day of home-grown programmes that was expected of us but often twice that amount.

One legacy of those years has been the enduring controversy about 'censorship' in the television coverage of the Northern Ireland conflict. A number of writers and programme-makers, mainly London-based, have complained that they were not allowed to broadcast what they wished, that the government pulled strings to silence them or that the broadcasting organizations themselves shelved or bowdlerized programmes for fear of causing controversy. As a result, they claim, the British public was denied the truth or at least part of the truth about what was going on. Most of this debate has revolved around the BBC, which does not concern me, but some of it relates to ITV and to Ulster Television. I must tackle that.

Early in the Troubles I had to establish the principle that we at Ulster Television should view in advance any potentially contentious programme dealing with Northern Ireland which was to be broadcast on ITV. The reason was straightforward: anything carried on the network would be seen in Northern Ireland and we would be the ones who would bear the responsibility locally for any consequences. And we had to pay for them! It followed that we had to know about it and to be able to advise, criticize or object where appropriate. We did not seek the right to veto any programme for UK showing – only the ITA had that power. Of course we could refuse to show a given programme in Northern Ireland but that was a last resort – I thought it was wrong for Ulster people to be given a different picture of events on their doorstep from that shown to the rest of the United Kingdom. So we settled for the right to view programmes in advance and say our tuppence-worth and we saw scores of programmes on that basis over the years. This procedure, I know, aroused suspicion and resentment because some journalists and programme-makers saw us as censors, but I make no apology for it.

Several concerns were in our minds when we watched such programmes and the first was the danger of violence: we knew well that programmes could inflame local opinion, bring rioters on to the street and possibly even provoke shootings or bombings. We also knew that a programme, while it might not directly cause bloodshed, could contribute to the climate of danger. Sometimes, of course, journalism requires the risk of doing all of those things because people need to be told the truth, and we knew all about this, too. One instance was the shocking film we had of Bloody Sunday, which we broadcast promptly and without hesitation. Another came in the aftermath of the Oxford Street bus station bomb in Belfast in 1972, part of the 'Bloody Friday' carnage. We acquired still pictures that day which were so horrific that a worried programme controller came to me for the decision about whether they should be screened; I told him to go ahead but to give viewers a warning first. More complex were the choices we had to make about extreme opinions. It would plainly have been wrong to exclude these on principle because we would have been presenting a false, 'disneyfied' world, but it would have been equally wrong to give them air time as a matter of course. Just because somebody says something outrageous or provocative, even if the speaker is a person of importance, it does not necessarily follow that those words should be broadcast, particularly if they may contribute to hatred or violence. It may be nothing more than deliberate trouble-making or attention seeking. We at Ulster Television gained experience in making judgments about these things and striking appropriate balances.

We were also worried about accuracy, and here I must speak bluntly. Much coverage of Northern Ireland by ITN and by ITV documentary-makers was intelligent and well-informed but some was not. 'Firemen', or general reporters, would sometimes arrive in Belfast at short notice and with little or no background knowledge. They might stay a few weeks, seeing nothing of the place beyond its principal battlegrounds and the interiors of the Europa Hotel and the Crown Bar, and then depart - never to return. During and after such a visit their qualification to comment on Ulster affairs, and their breadth of perspective, was limited to say the least and yet they often spoke on screen as though they were experts. Documentary researchers could be even worse - eager and immature they were almost parachuted into Belfast sometimes with just a few days to find a subject, master the background and set up a programme. Most of these people came to Havelock House and we fell over backwards to help them with contacts and a variety of local knowledge but it was not enough and again and again the programmes we viewed contained factual problems. When we pointed these out we were usually thanked and the mistakes were corrected but disputes arose and sometimes we endured arrogance and condescension.

I remember viewing a *Weekend World* programme on the night before transmission in company with, among others, the IBA's regional officer of the time, Tony Fleck. We had a telephone link with one of the producers in London and we were not happy with some factual matters. I said my piece and passed over to Tony, who endorsed my opinions forcibly. The argument continued until the London voice, clearly affronted, announced portentously: 'I'll have you know, Mr Fleck, that I am a very distinguished journalist.' His name was John Birt; at that time he must have been almost out of his 20s.

It might be said that giving Ulster Television its say on network programmes in this way was allowing the tail to wag the dog, for Northern Ireland accounted for just 3 per cent of the U.K. population and the British public had a right to be informed about what was going on. But there was an alternative perspective in which we, as the people directly affected by these events on a daily basis, could be seen as the dog, and the British public, who were spectators, as the tail. I do not say that either view was right or wrong but that both had to be kept in mind.

We did not take our responsibilities lightly. Programmes were usually viewed by at least three Ulster Television executives, of whom I was normally one and the other two were selected with care. If there was a fear that a programme would offend Protestants, then Protestant colleagues would be involved; if the concern was for Catholic feelings, then I ensured that Catholic colleagues were present. My own position, of course, often excited comment in familiar terms. Was I not a *News Letter* Henderson, a chip off the Unionist block? I have already explained how foolishly inaccurate this assumption was, but my efforts to dispel it never quite succeeded. To me the proof of the pudding was in the eating. Although Ulster Television racked up hundreds of complaints over the years from viewers in Northern Ireland, they were equally balanced. We never acquired a reputation for favouring one side over the other and our viewing figures, consistently higher than the BBC's, indicated that we retained the affection of the mass of the local population whatever their religion or politics.

What was the effect of our contribution in previewing sensitive programmes? I maintain that we saved ITV from many errors of fact and some of judgment but we did not distort or skew the coverage of the Troubles. On one occasion in the early days we dug our heels in over a pair of network offerings, the first of which gave a nationalist view of the Troubles and the second a unionist view. The makers insisted that the two programmes balanced each other, which in a strict sense they did, but we pointed out that they were to be broadcast a week apart, and so for a week only one view would have been seen, which in Ulster was a long time. It is a measure of how little our qualms were understood in London that they then offered to switch the programmes around, putting the unionist view first, in the belief that we would be happier with that. Of course we were not. Our rule was that there should be balance *within each programme,* in the sense that the views of both 'sides' should be reflected, and we said that balance *within a series* was not enough since it left time for feelings to be inflamed. In the end the two programmes were shown in the rest of Britain but not in Northern Ireland. A different problem arose over a programme made by Granada about the activities of a family of criminals in Belfast who had been involved in a couple of murders. This was presented in the programme as an aspect of the Troubles, as though the family were attached to a cause, but it was so ill-informed and misguided that even the engineers at our preview laughed it out of court. I agreed with them and we expressed our views to the IBA. Another Granada programme, *South of the Border,* caused probably the most famous, or infamous, controversy over censorship at ITV. Made, and banned, in 1971, this was an investigation of the IRA and contained interviews with people who could not be seen or identified, apparently spoken to in the Republic. We expressed some concerns but the decision to ban it, which caused outrage at Granada and considerable argument inside the IBA, was taken by the Authority on legal grounds.

We were never censors and we did not cheat the public of the truth. Rather, we tried to be informed and honest broadcasters in difficult and unprecedented circumstances. Our critics seem to have had a tenuous grasp of what was involved and at times they seemed to act and speak irresponsibly. I learned the hard way that – for all the brave talk of 'freedoms', 'rights' and 'principles' – there was no clear path for television, no simple set of guidelines to be followed. Usually my choice was not between the right way of doing something and the wrong way but between a variety of options each of which was bound to be wrong in some respect. The 'least wrong' choice was an anxious and often lonely business.

11
Still Growing

The mid-1970s saw the Troubles enter a different phase. Street rioting gave way to the bomb and the bullet and political instability and uncertainty were though to be replaced by Direct Rule. For Ulster Television this was a period of more challenges. Much had changed since those first days of covering protests and counter-protests in 1968. We were in colour, a gradual transition completed when our upgraded studio production facilities came fully on stream in 1972, enabling us to show not only recorded programmes but also the regular live shows such as *UTV Reports* in colour. We were more experienced; we had weathered covering crises from internment to the collapse of Stormont and from Bloody Sunday to the Ulster Workers' Council strike and we had produced a host of special programmes of all kinds, some of them broadcast on the network. And this was not at the cost of neglecting other local programme strands, where we were steadily gaining in ability and breadth. Perhaps 1977 marks a watershed in this story; two special events of that year stand out in my memory.

The first was the ordination of Tomas O'Fiaich as Catholic Archbishop of Armagh and Primate of Ireland. The previous Archbishop, Cardinal Conway, was a kindly, shy man and I had come to like him. (I remember his gratitude when I introduced him to the Presbyterian Moderator at Havelock House – he said afterwards: 'If I had not met that man here I might never have met him.') The appointment of O'Fiaich to succeed him was greeted with general surprise – he had been principal of Maynooth College and not even a bishop. I invited him to visit Ulster Television and this came very promptly. He was lively and cheerful and after a tour of the premises we adjourned to the boardroom for a chat. 'Would you like tea,' I inquired, 'or something else?' The answer was firm:

'Something else.' The Bushmills was opened, a useful session followed and we became friends. His ordination ceremony was a milestone for us, a long, full-blooded outside broadcast of a kind we had not previously been equipped to handle. I was in the congregation, sitting alongside Cecil Taylor of the BBC, which was also carrying it live. The new Archbishop spoke in no fewer than seven languages and was required on a few occasions to prostrate himself (a difficult task for a portly man to complete without loss of dignity), and it all ran considerably over time. For us this was no problem since the next programme due on ITV was an easily-postponed repeat of *Upstairs Downstairs*, but the BBC was in difficulty. Cecil, after many anxious glances at his watch, whispered urgently to me that he needed to leave to discuss what should be done. We were tightly packed and the atmosphere was solemn so I warned against it. 'These are sacred moments,' I said, but he had to go. With as little fuss as I could manage I let him out into the aisle where, to the glares of the congregation and with each footstep echoing to the rooftops, he made his way out of the cathedral to decide whether to pull the plug on the ceremony or on the BBC's forthcoming network programme.

The other major outside broadcast event of that year was the Queen's silver jubilee visit to Northern Ireland. Given the political climate of the time visits by any members of the Royal family were rare and for security reasons we were given only 12 days' notice that the Queen was coming. For the same reasons it had also been decided that she should not come to Belfast or Derry but that the trip would take in two 'safe' venues: Hillsborough Castle and the New University of Ulster in Coleraine. Since this offered very limited opportunities to those who wished to see her I thought that Ulster Television should supply proper coverage. At Hillsborough the main event was a garden party, which we were able to cover with an array of fixed cameras, but after that we had to dismantle the whole affair and rush everything to Coleraine. Given the extraordinarily tight security and the inevitable bomb hoaxes it was something of a miracle that we pulled it off. We carried 10 hours of live coverage over the two days, anchored by the incomparable Alastair Burnet, then the star of ITN and our Derek Murray. Alastair and I had been friends since trainee days in Glasgow. He came to my office on the evening before the visit for a chat and a drink. He wanted to pick my brains, for since I had been brought up in Hillsborough Castle when it was Government House and also had an intimate acquaintance with the New University, I had the background that he needed. Sure enough, in the occasional *longueurs* of the days that followed, I heard him trot out my memories as if they were his own. Alastair was a supreme broadcaster. ITN and Scottish Television – through golfing connections – did the stuff for us.

One hitch related to the Queen's lunch. It was a convention of royal life that the monarch was never shown on television in the act of eating, so when Her Majesty sat down to the formal luncheon in Coleraine we turned the cameras off. We were eager, however, to go back on air afterwards to capture the speeches by the Queen and others and on the basis of rehearsals involving stand-ins (another echo of my childhood) we were told that these speeches would start at 2 p.m.. This fell neatly after the end of *Crown Court*, a popular half-hour series. All was going well and the courtroom drama was unfolding in the normal way when at 1.45 p.m. we received the message from Coleraine that the Queen was rising to her feet. She was early. Suddenly I faced the choice Cecil Taylor had encountered in Armagh: should I pull the plug on the scheduled programme or on the outside broadcast? Record the Queen, I said, and we can show her speech as soon as Crown Court ends. By the skin of our teeth we got away with it, for the speech finished just in time for a dextrous engineer to rewind the tape and play it at 2 p.m. The hiccup had been caused by a simple error: the stand-in at the rehearsals was a heartier eater than Her Majesty.

Perhaps the greatest novelty of the royal visit was a documentary we commissioned from a Manchester producer called *A Day to Remember*. This was the Cinderella story of a young girl's day out to see the Queen, a project negotiated with the Palace at short notice. The Queen gave permission, then unique, for her voice to be heard in informal conversation with school children who swelled the enthusiastic crowd.

Just as the political climate in Northern Ireland changed in the later 1970s, we at Ulster Television felt the need to change our approach. The audience was exhausted and we had become a little stale. *UTV Reports* in particular, although still slick and professional and still the preferred evening news programme of the Northern Ireland public, had become formulaic, as though its makers had merely to turn the handle every day for it to come out. I felt that something new was required. Few things last in television - the public is fickle and the producers can easily fall into a rut, so sooner or later every series must be replaced. Popular staples such as *Romper Room* and *Teatime with Tommy* had long since gone and by 1977-78 it was the turn of *UTV Reports*. My thoughts turned back to the lighter sort of magazine we had delivered in *Roundabout*, but this time I wanted a programme lasting a whole hour, blending hard local news with softer human interest matters. The idea was ambitious - again, nobody in ITV was making such a programme - but it began to make real sense for us when Brian Waddell had the brilliant notion of hiring Gloria Hunniford to present it.

The blonde teenager who had declined my career advice in 1959 was by the late 1970s a well-established star in Northern Ireland, with her own successful BBC radio show, *A Taste of Hunni*. Brian advised me that she would cost more than our normal rates, but the more I thought about it the surer I was that she was the right person for us. Not only did she have the popularity to attract viewers but she also had the poise and the wit needed for an unpredictable live programme, and above all the ability to infuse it with a distinctive 'feel'. We made her an offer, she accepted and thus was born *Good Evening Ulster*, which went on air at the beginning of 1979. It was a runaway success to top everything we had done before, an exciting nightly rollercoaster of hard news and showbiz interviews, campaigns and competitions, revelations, humour and musical interludes. Gloria was sensational and this was not just a matter of talent and glamour but also of hard work, for the demands were relentless. I often bumped into her in the car park at 8 a.m. and her mind was already bubbling over with ideas, not only for that evening's programme but for the next day's and for others a week ahead and more. She did many specials – about jobs, about consumer affairs, about the Belfast Festival – but I especially remember an hour-long show she presented at the time the first DeLorean cars came off the production line in Dunmurry. All points of view were represented and all aspects explored – the famous car was parked in the middle of the studio – and to cap it all she conducted an excellent interview with John DeLorean himself. It was first-class television.

While the thinking behind *Good Evening Ulster* owed much to the changing mood of the times, another factor played its part: the licence. The years 1979-80 brought to ITV another of those painful spasms caused by the periodic reviews of the broadcasting contracts. Our last experience had been in 1968-69, when Lord Hill threw his spanners into the works (although happily he left Ulster Television alone). Now there was another in the offing and I was aware well in advance that for the first time since we launched we would have a challenger. *Good Evening Ulster* was a weapon in this contest; we were showing our strength.

Before dealing with that contest I should first paint in a little background and one element of that was the arrival of commercial radio. From the moment this was first discussed I believed that we should be involved. Of course it was a business proposition but it was also vital to gain local parity with the BBC, which was allowed to broadcast on both media. Just as they did on BBC (only rather better, I hoped) we could share resources between radio and television and at the same time cross-promote, plugging television programmes on the radio and vice versa. A radio station supported by us, I thought, would have a far better chance of competing as an equal with BBC Radio in Northern Ireland. I did not suggest that the new radio company should be a mere subsidiary of Ulster Television – on the contrary, Basil Lapworth and I constructed a consortium which was quite distinct. Both UTV's shareholding and my own were to be at a minimum, while the station was to have its own premises on the Ormeau Road. In the chair was Charles Adams, an accountant and a leading supporter of classical music and opera in Northern Ireland, while backing him were Mervyn Solomon, a businessman with expertise in the popular music world, and George Lavery, who had been a member of the Scarman Tribunal which investigated the Troubles of 1968 and 1969. We wrote what I thought was an impressive and unusual bid which, among other things, made a virtue of creative and financial links with UTV. Unfortunately, when the contracts were awarded in 1975 we were unsuccessful. Although Lord Aylestone, who had succeeded Hill as ITA chairman, praised it as the best submission he had seen, for reasons which I considered wrongheaded the Authority had determined that the radio station should have no connection with us. It would be 'unseemly for Ulster Television to have its feet under the table', we were told. Instead the contract went to a rival group backed by the *Belfast Telegraph* (which in turn was owned by the Thomson Organisation, proprietors of the *Times* and the *Sunday Times* – somehow they were allowed to have their feet under the table despite their Scottish Television and radio interests). I was sore about the outcome but I bore no grudge against Downtown Radio, as the station came to be known. After encountering great difficulties and long delays they went on to do a fine job and provide a good news service.

By the later 1970s, when our own contract was coming up for renewal, Lord Aylestone had been replaced as chairman by Lady Plowden. Before she came to us her experience in broadcasting had been acquired at the BBC where she had been deputy chairman and where she may have picked up her enthusiasm for the worthy and the dull and also some of her authoritarian ways. The peerless Robert Fraser had retired so Lady Plowden's director general was a different character, Brian Young, who had made his mark as a young head of Charterhouse School and at the Nuffield Foundation. Handsome and intellectual, Young had a fresh mind. We all liked him – at the start. These two, Plowden and Young, made a peculiar partnership. They created in common a tedious and damaging obsession with public service programmes and other dreary forms of broadcasting but Young was more realistic and this may have explained the curious tensions between them. I remember one morning in London making my way across Hyde Park towards the IBA offices and spotting Lady Plowden striding along ahead of me at top speed. With some difficulty I caught up and fell in step, eager to show that I too was an early morning person full of purpose and vigour. After a while I felt compelled to ask why we were walking so fast, to which she replied distractedly: 'I must get to the office before Brian.'

These, then, were the principal hands on the tiller at the IBA when, at the end of the 1970s, the time came to decide the future of Ulster Television. Our challengers called themselves Northern Ireland Independent Television, or NIITV, and were led by none other than Lord Dunleath, who (the attentive reader will recall) had briefly been one of the aristocrats in our own team back in 1958. On that occasion he had withdrawn. In the interval he had served as a BBC governor and Chairman of the Alliance Party from which post he resigned to take on the chair of NIITV. Their managing director was to be another man well known to us: Derek Bailey. Derek had started at Ulster Television as a floor manager in the early days but he was too big a talent to keep and though he returned twice – once to produce *Flashpoint* – he was soon enjoying deserved success in London. Also in their team was Denis Tuohy, who had worked both at the BBC and at Thames and who hailed originally from Northern Ireland. Behind these men was an array of 'names' designed to impress both in Ulster and London: James Galway, Phil Coulter, Frank Carson, Seamus Heaney, Mary Peters and the like. That some of these, and others involved, had not only been friends of Ulster Television over the years but also, as I thought, friends of *mine* was a little difficult to swallow but Northern Ireland is a small place.

It was a life-or-death battle, for defeat would mean the end of Ulster Television as a business. Since that was not acceptable I planned and fought the strongest campaign I could possibly manage. Everything I had learned in 20 years, every ounce of influence, every insight and every contact, was directed to that end. We fought fair but we fought hard, though it was difficult to ignore the absurd claims made by some in our opposing camp.

My natural view was that, given our record, there should never have been any question of displacing Ulster Television. The manner in which we had coped with the extraordinary demands of the Troubles, which was something that no other ITV company, large or small, ever had to confront, should alone have assured us of a renewed licence. And against the background of division and civil unrest we had not only maintained our general service but also expanded it considerably so that we consistently outperformed the BBC in the local ratings. Nor had the business climate been uniformly favourable, for in the same years there had been at least two recessions, each of which bit hard into our revenues. And as if life had not been difficult enough, we had endured a long period when our annual IBA rental and network programme changes were exceptionally and unfairly high – our complaints were vindicated when they were eventually reduced. In short the company had more than met its public service obligations while at the same time proving that it was competently and prudently managed. What more could the IBA want?

In crude terms the answer was that tradition demanded changes in the contractors. Normally one big company, one middling one and one small one were axed in each round, and after 20 years there seemed every chance that our turn might have come. Of course there were other issues at stake and I found to my dismay that one of them was me. As the IBA's own official history records, there was a perception in some influential quarters that Ulster Television had become a one-man band with Brum Henderson as that one man. Not that I was doing everything myself – the idea is absurd – but that I held too many of the policy strings. In particular it was noted that for a while after 1976 I operated without a programme controller of the kind employed at most other stations, and that I was discharging most of those functions myself. I was therefore running the business as managing director as well as shaping the programme output and this was somehow seen as bad for the company or for the audience.

Much better to keep the roles separate, they thought at the IBA, partly because this would generate 'creative tension' (a fashionable business phrase of the time). I never accepted this. Yes, I resisted pressure to appoint a programme controller, partly because the right candidate had not appeared and partly because I felt comfortable (though busy) discharging those functions. There was a harmony with my other functions and, in particular, there was no adverse impact on our programmes. On the contrary, because I understood the state of the business I could give a more effective lead on the programme side – we operated within our means and we were in tune with our audience. Some people forgot that I was not one of the breed of grey television executives then beginning to take over; I had a background in the arts and journalism and so had plenty to contribute on the programme side, and in a company as small as ours it made sense to do so. As for 'creative tension', besides being a foolish and destructive notion in the first place (did we not have enough tension already in Northern Ireland?) it was a needlessly expensive one. Despite all of this I have no doubt that suspicions about me and resentment at the way I defied the IBA on this issue played their part in the events of 1979 and 1980.

Our positive case for a fresh contract was powerful, but I also made sure that several important developments came to fruition at the most apposite time. Havelock House was enlarged by a new production complex and workshop, while at the same time we bought a state-of-the-art outside broadcast unit and for the first time established a studio and offices in Derry – all evidence that we were both expanding and coming closer to the people of Northern Ireland. *Good Evening Ulster*, now getting into its stride, offered further proof of this, for it was not only an ambitious programme but also a substantial expansion of our weekly output. Its success was a powerful card in our hand. In one week, I recall, all five instalments of *Good Evening Ulster* were in the ten most highly-rated local programmes on BBC or ITV in Northern Ireland. This would be difficult if not impossible for our NIITV rivals to match. We played some more subtle cards, too. In the crucial period I was serving as president of the Northern Ireland Chamber of Commerce, addressing business meetings, lunches and dinners in every county and town, as well as in London, and I am not embarrassed to say that I made full use of these opportunities to remind people of the strengths of Ulster Television. And 1980 also happened to be the year of our 21st birthday. Our 20th had come and gone without much fanfare, but with contract renewal in the air we chose to mark our 21st with a number of high-profile events, culminating in a gala evening at the Grand Opera House in Belfast. In the same period we unveiled two important production projects, the first a two-hour film of the life, times and music of Percy French and the second an idea known as 'Project Slipper' which had been discussed since the earliest days of Ulster Television. It was to prove our most ambitious undertaking to date, taking several more years to bring to fruition and requiring me, in the American phrase, to 'bet the farm'. Project Slipper was *The Irish R.M.*

The Somerville and Ross stories of a bewildered English magistrate at the mercy of a canny and eccentric Irish country community in the 19th century were perfect material for a television drama series. The stories were told in distinct episodes but with a sustained cast of central characters. They were lively, witty and charming and were distinctly Irish. William MacQuitty had originally bought the option on the television rights and annually I had renewed it but we lacked the resources and the experience in drama to proceed with a series on such a scale. In the late 1970s, however, I was approached at a programme sales conference in Cannes by the producer James Mitchell who wanted to know whether the rights were for sale or whether we would consider backing him to make a series. The plan was to produce six one-hour dramas for national television, with two further series of six to follow if the first was successful. I could see the value of such a series in our bid for a new contract but the costs were daunting – the bill for a single series would be much greater than Ulster Television's entire annual profit. Of course we could not carry the whole risk ourselves so the first phase of the operation, once we decided to press ahead with Mitchell as producer, was finding partners. After long and complicated negotiations this was achieved: Rediffusion supported us, as did WGBH of Boston, while the embryonic Channel 4 undertook to broadcast the series nationally once they went on air. RTE, for their part, gave technical help. Even so the risks for us remained astronomical and we would only recoup our investment if the series was a success and if we could sell it afterwards abroad.

The final dimension of our contest with NIITV was a series of IBA roadshows and debates up and down Northern Ireland – Plowden and Young were enthusiasts for public meetings. Most of my senior colleagues were involved but I took the leading role and Gloria was a vigorous supporter, often leaving the studio after her show at 7 p.m. and driving directly to join us on the campaign trail. Lord Antrim, sadly, was no longer with us, having died in 1977, so our Chairman at the time was James MacQuitty. To the dismay of the IBA the turnouts were often poor and the debates flat. Our critics were often glib and impractical, with too little grasp of all that we had done and tried to do, and had to say so. I also resented the way in which we were portrayed as low-brow which we were able to show was a caricature of our output. It was easy to find fault with a complicated business and easier still to 'jazz up' a case with celebrity backers but what mattered was our delivery over the years.

These exercises caused much friction but resolved little and inevitably it was the interviews with the IBA in London which decided the issue. The Authority clearly wanted to challenge us on the one-man band issue, so instead of turning up with the usual bevy of non-executive directors all the senior management came demonstrating in the flesh that we had more talent in depth than mine and that I was not running the show alone. In the end we won and NIITV was defeated. The Authority said of Ulster Television: 'Their record in a difficult area and their ability to form an effective rapport with the viewers of the province were considerable factors in this decision.' Inevitably, they also used the occasion for more meddling, in particular looking for the promise of long-term changes in the company's management structure. They were not losing the chance to divide and conquer.

Not long after these events one of the minor highlights of my life occurred: I had lunch with the Queen. Exactly what prompted the invitation at that time I was not told and still do not know for sure, but I suspect it was connected with my role at the Royal Television Society. I had been on the society's council for a few years (another string to my contract renewal bow) when I found myself elected national Chairman a job demanding considerable vigour. I was determined to rejuvenate what was becoming a rather grey membership. It was as this term was drawing to an end that the call came from Buckingham Palace: would I be available for a small private lunch with Her Majesty? Of course I was. The caller then referred to my background and my father's position and expressed confidence that I would be 'all right' so far as protocol was concerned. I said I hoped that would be the case.

The occasion, when it came, passed for the most part in a haze of good manners and courtesy. I scarcely remember who the other guests were – they included a table tennis player and a clergyman, I think – and I was not conscious of what we ate and drank, except that it was all very pleasant. There were eight of us and the Queen and Prince Philip were everything that hosts should be – affable, attentive, interested and interesting. Everyone there seemed as involved in the conversations as I did. When the meal ended and the party broke up, something truly unexpected happened: I found myself alone with the Queen for a private chat lasting 15 minutes. Clearly this too was part of the Palace plan but again I have no idea how or why it came about. What I do know – and this part I remember vividly – is that it was both fascinating and revealing. We discussed ITV, of which the Queen had a remarkable knowledge, to the point that she was aware not only of current problems in the industry but also of others still on the horizon. And she was not merely going through the motions, for when I offered my thoughts she responded with views and observations of her own, fully engaging with me on the subject. Then she turned to the Budget which Sir Geoffrey Howe had just delivered, and gave me a full and enlightening commentary on it. Finally we talked about Northern Ireland and it was then, as the conversation was coming to an end and Prince Philip came in to join us, that she said to me: 'Mr Henderson, I am told you do an impression of Mr Paisley.' I was taken aback but could not deny that I did. 'Perhaps you would do it for us now,' said the Queen. It was a Royal command so I obliged. Although it would be wrong of me to repeat a certain remark she made, she evidently liked it for a few months later I heard that someone else from Northern Ireland who had been invited to the Palace had been told by the Queen that I did a 'fine imitation of Ian Paisley'.

Before that day I had never been an anti-monarchist but nor had I been enthusiastic about the Crown. The encounter, however, left me with a powerful impression of the Queen's intellect and insight. That she should be well-informed is hardly surprising; she can surround herself with bright and efficient people. But that she should have such a shrewd command of the information she is given, that she can discuss its implications with such authority and wisdom certainly took me by surprise. We see her usually in her role as figurehead, shaking hands, opening events and making small talk. I left the Palace that afternoon convinced that she was a far more substantial and perhaps more powerful figure than most of us imagine.

12
A Good Walk – Enhanced

On a wall of my County Down home there hangs a handsome, hand-crafted putter mounted upon a stand and bearing the inscription: 'Dedicated to Brum Henderson, whose golfing career was interrupted by television.' Like most good jokes this one has truth in it for, although I have never been a good player (my lowest handicap was 10) I have always loved the game. Despite the inscription I found opportunities to combine business with the pleasure of the course, to the advantage of Ulster Television.

Golf has been described famously as 'a good walk spoiled'. Rubbish. It is the best walk combining seriousness and fun which is unique and often extremely pleasant. Certainly there is a good walk, and there are real joys in a day spent in the open air amidst countryside and scenery often the finest to be found. The company is usually good – friendly people in attractive places – but the zest lies in the game. First and foremost one plays against oneself and there is an irresistible compulsion to improve this, correct that and sometimes to experiment a little. At the same time there is always a risk: one lapse of concentration can mar four hours of work and waste all the practice and planning. So golfers are always on their mettle. All golfers like to win but the real pleasure lies in rivalry for excellence with friends as in straight competition with them. We count the strokes or the holes won, but we also commend opponents' fine putts, lucky escapes, brave drives and so forth. A man can win soundly and still share the pleasure of his rival's improved performance or his plucky recovery from a bad start. Golf is also a revelation of character; one learns a lot about a rival from the way he handles setbacks and pressure on the golf course as well as from his response to victory and defeat. In the end, though, golf is simply *agreeable*. I have always found the mornings of golfing days to be happy times as I contemplate the pleasures of the course while shaving and ponder what clothes to wear to fit the conditions, and any business that has to be conducted first is always done in a glow of good humour. I started young but it was not until later in life that I came to enjoy such days with regularity and that is another important debt I owe to my wife Pat.

Golf runs in the family. Uncle James was a plus two player and a leading figure in the sport in Ireland, and his gift was such that I was somewhat overawed. A smallish man with a stoop, James never managed more than 170 yards off the tee but what he lacked in distance he made up for in accuracy. Every drive was dead straight and, in the words of the great Fred Daly (of whom more in a moment), 'straight is worth 20 yards'. Within 100 yards of the flag James was deadly, holing out in two with daunting regularity and ease. The high point of his playing career came in 1922 when he was honorary secretary of the Golfing Union of Ireland and also had to organise the Northern Ireland Open Amateur competition. Finding that there were 87 entrants when the lists closed, he added his own name to make 22 four-balls for the eliminating rounds. This meant that he was not only running the event but also playing in it, That was not all for he was providing full reports at every stage for the *News Letter*, his paper. None of this prevented him from progressing smoothly through the rounds to the final, at which point he received a telegram from the paper saying: 'Congratulations on reaching final STOP Am sending reporter to cover STOP Good luck STOP Signed Editor'. To this James replied: 'Do not waste money STOP Will cover own final STOP Who owns this newspaper STOP Signed J.H.' In the event he was beaten six and five by Alfie Lowe of the Malone club and his report for the News Letter included the splendidly objective observation: 'At the 23rd Henderson's nerve cracked.'

For me, golf began on the number two course, or 'Hen Run', now called the Annesley links, at Newcastle, County Down. Dad, Mum, Bill and I would spend a 'family fortnight' at the Slieve Donard Hotel, which in those days had privileges with the Royal County

Down, and so we boys were introduced early to the joys of the game. Despite Uncle James's impatience with my early, clumsy efforts, I was soon hooked. At first it was mainly a holiday pursuit, particularly in wartime when both golf balls and money were in short supply, although I remember cycling from Hillsborough to Lisburn occasionally to play on the course there. In those days it was simplicity itself: off with the coat, loosen the tie and wear ordinary rubber-soled shoes – and of course it never seemed to rain. My school, Bradfield, favoured team games but even there, as I have described, I seized every opportunity to slip away to Calcot by bicycle for a round and I remember vividly one game there. I was captain of the school team when we played the old boys – or the Old Bradfieldian Golfing Society, to give them their full title – and was pitted against their captain, one James Cumming who was a former colonel in the Scots Guards and a scratch golfer. I had my hands full, but managed to give a reasonable account of myself and was still only two down when we reached the 17th, a short hole played over water and up to a green beside an enormous tree. I landed just short of the hole and was congratulating myself on staying in contention when his ball popped down on to the green, squarely between mine and the hole. I shot a glance at him but he was stony-faced and silent: these were the days of stymies, so both balls stayed where they were. Now I had a choice: I could give him the hole lose or try to play myself out of it. I chose the bold course, picked out my trusty niblick, a lovely wooden shaft with a lead head and suede handle, and lined up. The shot was extraordinarily difficult but to my astonishment – and Cumming's – the ball jumped clean over his, dropped down on the far side and rolled towards the hole. If it had only caught the edge of the cup it might have gone in, but alas it did not. I paid further for my effrontery as Cumming ruthlessly demolished the final hole in two shots, an immense drive followed by a rifled approach which sank for a birdie on a difficult par four.

(In due course I became a member of the Old Bradfieldian Golfing Society myself and many years later was proud to support the creation of a beautiful course within the school grounds, designed by

Donald Steel. One of the nine holes, a tricky par four, was named in honour of the four Bradfield Hendersons – my father, uncle Lilburn, Bill and myself – and I went back to take part in the opening tournament on a course which might one day, perhaps, produce a young champion.)

By the age of 19 I was lucky enough to be selected with three other Ulster boys for special instruction with the Golf Foundation which sought new talent. We gathered at the Belvoir Park Golf Club in south Belfast where our instructor was none other than Fred Daly, the only man from Ireland to win the Open and an Ulsterman to the fingertips of his amazingly broad but very stubby hands. Fred was a true character as well as a great golfer and we met often in the years which followed. Those hands of his, with the assistance of only a two iron, could with ease propel a ball 220 yards straight as a die. Not only did he win the Open in 1947 but he was twice runner-up and his figures in the competition are a phenomenon: in 20 rounds played over five years his average score was 70. That day at Belvoir, therefore, he was at the height of his powers and laid on a dazzling demonstration, briskly playing six holes in four under par using only that trusty two iron, before turning to some serious, high-quality teaching. It all boiled down to his seven famous words: 'Still head, turn hips, hands through ball.' And if we couldn't remember those he said three would do 'alright': 'Head behind ball.'

Fred later was a very popular President of the Belfast Press Golf Society, of which I was a member, and in 1987 we decided to honour him by taking him back to the scene of his triumph 40 years earlier at Royal Liverpool. On the ferry I remember this modest man chatting about his days at the top, when prize money was small (he received just £250 for winning the Open) and times were hard for players without alternative incomes. He and his old friend and rival, Harry Bradshaw, travelled on a shoestring to take part in competitions all around Britain and Ireland, often turning up at a club by bus or on foot only to be sent around to the back door where 'someone would look after them'. Unknown to Fred, we had arranged for Harry to be present at Hoylake for the anniversary and

Fred was putting on the green when Harry tapped him on the shoulder saying: 'How are you, Fred?' 'Jaysus, is it yourself?' came the reply, to which Harry said: 'It's not Jaysus, it's me.' Long, happy reminiscences followed, in which two old friends happily seemed to forget that anyone else was present.

Fred was blunt, as we were reminded that night. The members of the Royal Liverpool, splendidly attired in red tail coats and white ties, laid on a fine dinner and the club captain made a speech which did great justice to Fred's many achievements. Nevertheless, when Fred rose to his feet he repaid the compliment by analyzing in detail the changes made to the Hoylake course since 1947 and concluding with unsparing honesty that on balance they were for the worse. He was, in fact, a golfing conservative and I remember his bitter feelings on another occasion, when continental players were finally included in the Ryder Cup teams to play the United States. Addressing a dinner at Bangor Golf Club, Fred, not usually given to strong language, made a series of unprintable remarks about various European nationalities before asking: 'Why in the name of God can the buggers not pick a crowd of decent British and Irish boys and get bate by the Americans like we always used to do?'

I have mentioned that I played a good deal at Trinity. The club there had about 30 members and I was secretary for a time, with responsibility for arranging matches with other clubs around Dublin. Since we had no course or clubhouse of our own it was important to ingratiate ourselves with our hosts and we were not above instructing some of our players to promote goodwill by losing – that way we would be asked back to drink their liquor, eat their food and entertain their ladies again the next year. Different in mood were our encounters with other universities, usually played at Royal Dublin, Portmarnock or Baltray. These could be dour, tense affairs, though we had an ace in our pack in the form of Peter Froggatt, now Sir Peter, who whittled his handicap down to low single figures, won a fistful of medals and eventually played for his country. Our captain was Charlie McCaw, a fine golfer himself who was a little concerned when the captain of Royal Dublin was soundly thrashed by Peter. We were 'encouraged' to leave.

In my *News Letter* days I played regularly but, as the inscription on that putter says, Ulster Television caused an interruption and I was restricted to the rare game, always with a business connection. One early example - and an illuminating one - comes from 1961, when I played against London advertising agents for the first time. We gathered at glorious Sunningdale, where the occasion began with a long and very liquid lunch, after which at the first tee we found a group of five deferential caddies. The extra one was pulling, not a set of clubs, but a drinks trolley. Before we started the stakes were declared - 'one, one, two' - meaning, as I understood it, a pound for the first nine, a pound for the second and two for the 18. Although I was used to playing for shillings I accepted the challenge reckoning that Ulster Television could afford my losses if things went badly. Not surprisingly, as the round progressed and the fifth caddy was kept busy the standard of golf deteriorated steadily but I discovered that I was keeping my head better than most. I was in for a surprise for as our little party staggered away from the 18th hole one of the agents thrust a large wad of fivers in my hand and declared: 'There you are, old boy, I hope your programmes are as good as your golf.' I had not won four pounds, but four hundred. It was just as well I had kept my head because, while no doubt these pleasant gentlemen were able to put their losses on expenses, the Board of Ulster Television would not have been quite so generous with me.

Another memorable early business outing took me to the opening of the Moyola Park course in Castledawson. This was on the estate of James Chichester-Clark, later briefly the Prime Minister of Northern Ireland, and his wife Moyra, and they had sought advice about it from a number of people, including Lennox Cotton one of our original shareholders. He encouraged me to persuade the Board to make a modest investment. I sought golfing privileges for there was only a slim prospect of a financial return, but Moyola could be a base for entertaining advertisers and advertising agents in agreeable circumstances. I played in one of the inaugural exhibition rounds with Christie O'Connor (Senior). This was a strange experience. From the first tee, in characteristic style, 'himself' propelled the ball some 260 yards into the dim distance while I followed with a modest 180-yarder. As I made my way up to my ball I looked forward and saw an admiring crowd around Christie's ball up ahead, oblivious to the fact that a mortal was also playing. There were no marshals and we were filming the event so somewhat uneasily, in fear that I was about to kill a spectator and ruin the whole occasion, I picked a seven iron and aimed over their heads. Fortunately the ball landed beyond them and I completed my round without disgrace. What impressed me most about Christie that day was his hard head. His wife had driven him 140 miles from Dublin. He accepted some Bushmills on arrival; at the turn he had more and two more followed in the clubhouse as we toasted his round. A little later at dinner he gave an excellent speech and downed several more. Finally, after one or two 'for the road', he took his leave and even then he was steady as a rock, with not a hint of wear and tear. This was impressive enough but the next morning when I rang to thank him for making the journey his wife informed me that he had been nursing a temperature of 101 degrees all that day.

His nephew, Christie Junior, played with me at another pro-am event some years later and proved most helpful and patient around the course, even though once again there was more at stake than I realized. At the 18th I put the ball eight foot from the pin after a drive and a six iron but my nerve failed and I foozled it to four feet. 'Sink it while you're hot,' said Christie, warmly, and somehow I managed it. With that he put his arm around my shoulder and announced: 'Thanks very much. You've just won me £1,000.' What possessed him to predict the result I will never know. Here again the encounter turned to advantage for over dinner I discovered that he had made no arrangements for staying the night. After clearing it first with my wife he came to stay at home and there followed a long night of stories about the golf tour, full of fascinating insights into the lives of the famous names. I was inspired, and the result was a successful Ulster Television series, *Golfing Greats*, featuring interviews with the likes of Nicklaus, Watson, Palmer, Player, Ballesteros, Sarazen and Snead.

Another golfing encounter was at Royal Portrush where the winner's prize was none other than the Isle of Man. My companion and adversary was Robin Gill, founder of Border Television, one of the smallest regional stations, based in Carlisle. Border went on air two years after Ulster Television and in the interval we came to learn about our experience. The Isle of Man lay neatly between the Ulster and Border regions and at that time the ITA had not decided in whose territory it fell, so I suggested to Robin jokingly that we settle the matter between ourselves; we should play for the right to the island. Those viewers would have been a welcome addition to our set count and a boost to our advertising revenue. When in due course he arrived on the Larne ferry I drove him up to Royal Portrush. Robin had been a rugby Blue at Oxford and turned out to be a solid golfer so the game was nip and tuck. After a couple of holes we came up behind a pair of Catholic priests who kindly waved us through, and as we passed I asked whether they might like to join us. They did, and both proved more adept than we were. Serious golf ensued and it was Robin's game which suffered. When the final ball sank I was ahead and I claimed my prize as we made for the clubhouse with our new companions. Alas for Ulster Television things did not work out that way since the final decision was not left to Robin and me. But the game was a happy fancy.

As I have said, a round of golf was a rarity in those days but however busy I was, even in the Troubles years, there was one annual golfing event never to be missed – because it was one that I dreamed up myself. This was the 'Natural Break'. The ITV companies were a loose federation with real relationships only at the higher levels and it occurred to me in 1962 that it would be good for the staffs of all the ITV companies if they could meet each other on different terms. Accordingly I commissioned a silver cup, to be called The Natural Break Trophy (a natural break was the moment in a television programme when the action halted in an apparently appropriate way to allow advertisements to be shown), and instituted an annual golfing competition. Initially we played only against Scottish Television (it was Bill Brown of Scottish who later gave me the handmade putter with the inscription) but soon I extended it to include all the companies and RTE as well. Staged in rotation, it roamed the courses and hotels of the British Isles, growing every year in scale and boisterousness until eventually as many as 150 golfers attended.

The character of these occasions may be judged from our experience in staging the Natural Break in 1970 when we chose the Great Northern Hotel in Bundoran as the venue. A great throng from all corners of the British Isles converged on Aldergrove, where a dinner was laid on with a superb speech of welcome at Aldergrove by Roy Bradford on behalf of the Northern Ireland government. (To general delight, he performed for us *his* excellent impression of Ian Paisley.) Coaches then whisked everyone west to County Donegal, making many pit stops along the way, and deposited the nervous party at various hotels for several hours sleep. Next morning the anglers and 'camp followers' departed in their various directions while the golfers divided into two groups, the better ones playing at Rosses Point and the rest on the hotel course. The competition was fierce, not least because the event tended to be sponsored by leading advertisers and the prizes on offer were so generous that they compromised our amateur status. (I recall one RTE engineer setting off home - not from Bundoran but in another year - with the equivalent of £1,000 in winnings.) In the evening, before and after dinner, the bar was busy to say the least and there was traditional music to help the drink down. One small group who gave us the slip were later found to have been drinking poteen in a local pub, to devastating effect. The revelry continued all weekend, punctuated at night by serious poker games at which I remember Leonard Parkin, the ITN newsreader, as a gracious loser. When, bleary-eyed but happy, we finally checked out to return to our homes and our offices, the management of the Great Northern informed us that never before in the history of the hotel had so much drink been sold in so short a time.

Such outings were the exception rather than the rule for me, which was probably just as well. It was not until 1977 that golf became, once again, more than an occasional distraction from work. Pat had the idea that it would do me good so, with that encouragement, I accepted the invitation of two boyhood friends, Charles Adams and Harry McCaw, to join the club where my golfing adventures had begun, Royal County Down. From then the historic links course at Newcastle, with its dipping dunes, its gorse thickets and its magnificent view of the Mourne Mountains became my therapy. After nearly 20 very hard years, with long hours and few breaks, it was sheer joy to spend a regular Saturday in the open air, pitting my wits against the course and enjoying that companionship which only fellow-golfers can provide. And this being such a sociable game I soon found myself invited to take part in a variety of pro-am events in Northern Ireland and further afield, which proved a fascinating introduction both to great golfers and to other players, famous and otherwise. Among my more unexpected companions have been Christopher Lee and Henry Cooper, while at a Bob Hope charity tournament at Moor Park I was paired with Douglas Bader, the celebrated fighter pilot who had lost both legs in a crash before the war. A bluff, businesslike character, Bader played surprisingly well given his disability but at the 14th tee he misjudged his swing and fell flat on his back. Tentatively – I was concerned about those tin legs becoming detached – I helped him up again, whereupon he shook himself, stamped his feet and barked: 'Damned stupid of me. Got legless at lunchtime.'

I enjoyed a run of luck in these pro-ams and in other competitions – because of my long lay-off my handicap was higher than it should have been, and it may have helped that I had become teetotal – so I picked up a number of prizes. No fewer than five decanters, for example, found their way on to the shelves at home and Pat watched their arrival with bemusement and, I thought, some small pride. Then on one occasion I came home empty-handed and she asked: 'Where is it?' 'Well I didn't win today,' I explained, a little wounded. 'But don't they always give you something anyway?' she replied. She had been under the impression that decanters were awarded simply for turning up and of this I was happy to disabuse her.

Pat herself soon began playing, although it took a holiday in Spain to win her over. I booked a trip that included access to the Rio Real club outside Marbella and there, on the magnificent greensward, beneath a perfect blue sky and golden sun – with the additional assistance of instruction from the great Angel Miguel – Pat succumbed. Thus the game became a shared pastime for us and over the years, particularly later when we bought a second home in Florida and joined the Royal Palm club there, we have enjoyed many a happy round together. Indeed I am proud that on my 60th birthday Pat and I won the mixed foursomes at Royal County Down and the following year completed an unusual double by winning a similar tournament at Royal Palm.

I was once warned by a lady friend of my parents that two things would wreck a marriage: the in-laws and the Royal County Down. I can see what she meant about the great Newcastle links for anyone who plays there can see why it has been rated among the top ten anywhere. It has become for me a place of happy memories. It was there that I asked Brian Mawhinney, then a minister at the Northern Ireland Office, to play. When he struck a ball into the deep rough at the 9th hole we heard a cry of pain and moments later a party of soldiers, fully armed and heavily camouflaged, stood up to reveal themselves – part of the minister's security protection.

There was another occasion when Royal County Down helped me land a tremendous deal for Ulster Television. With the lure of the great course I persuaded Dick Johnson, the advertisement director of Procter and Gamble, to come over for a day's golf and in the warm glow of satisfaction after the game he mentioned that his company – a hugely important television advertiser in Britain – was contemplating a test campaign for a new product. He inquired whether Ulster Television might be interested. Seemingly casually, since I was thrilled by the idea, I said that yes, we could take it. 'But you don't know about the product,' he said, a little sheepishly, to which I replied that we would take the campaign whatever he was selling. 'It's called Vortex,' he said, and I declared that it was sounding more exciting by the minute. 'It is a rival to Domestos,' he went on, 'You know … for cleaning lavatories.' 'Dick, I will be honest with you,' I declared. 'I would go anywhere to get a test campaign from Procter and Gamble, even around the hidden bend.' He laughed and was as good as his word; to the great envy of rivals from other regions we landed the Vortex test contract and in a year our whole business with P&G doubled. It was worth a million a year. The golf was enjoyable, too.

In 1985 Royal County Down invited me to write, in collaboration with Harry McCaw, a history of the club to appear in its centenary year, 1989. An infinitely more distinguished golfer than I, Harry had been one of the club's youngest captains and went on to be captain of the Royal and Ancient, too. My qualification, besides a background in the business of words, was a family one, for the only previous history had been written by my Uncle James. Between us Harry and I met our deadline but it involved a harder grind than had been envisaged, ploughing through records, drafting the text and tracing illustrations, not to mention organizing funds to cover the costs not only of the project but also of the centenary celebrations. Alarmingly, 'writer's block' visited me for the first time in my life and I suffered long periods of anxious struggle, but one wet day in Florida the creative juices suddenly flowed and in a single session from 8 a.m. to midnight I broke the back of the job. A bright idea was to recruit that fine cartoonist Rowel Friers to help. Once, in my *News Letter* days, I tried to poach Rowel from the *Belfast Telegraph* so we knew each other well. (His editor learned of my approach, doubled his cartoonist's pay and told me to mind my own business, so although I failed to capture Rowel he had reason to thank me for the attempt.) He contributed some delightful original golfing cartoons to our book, directly linked to the text, and these brightened the whole affair. To our great satisfaction the volume proved a hot seller and was quickly re-printed. Harry's 'feel' for golf is unique.

Over the years, besides being a proud member at Royal County Down, I joined some golfing societies which brought pleasure and entertainment in different measures. One was the NAGS, or the Newspapers and Advertisers Golfing Society. One of the oldest societies of its kind, with a collection of trophies so enormous that the

Hon Secretary needed a large car to transport them to tournaments. The NAGS was based at my own London club, the Naval and Military, and though I had been concerned about the vetting procedure it turned out that one of the selectors was an advertisers' agent I knew well, so I was admitted without ado. It was not a business club, by which I mean that deal-making and shop talk on the course were discouraged but the NAGS (the emblem on the tie is of course a horse) played on the best courses around London – Walton Heath, Sunningdale, the Berkshire and St George's Hill – and they had an annual outing to France. Other societies included the Old Bradfieldians and the Belfast Press Golf Society. It is not only the best golfers who achieve holes in one and I have been lucky enough to have five. It used to carry the obligation of buying drinks all round on the return to the clubhouse so it is a mixed blessing. Few golfers can have been so punished for their luck as I was on one of those occasions, when my little triumph occurred at Knock, with the Belfast Press Golf Society. Not only did the company include some competent drinkers but it was the Christmas outing so we were present in strength. The morning, moreover, had seen a ladies' competition, and since it was a Monday we were joined by a number of clergymen (it used to be common for men of the cloth to play golf on their 'day of rest'). The bar, then, was full to bursting and news of the hole in one had preceded me so I found myself standing the biggest drinks order of my life. The final bill was more than somewhat. Was it worth it? Absolutely.

13

Parting Company

We had promised *The Irish R.M.* in our application for the new IBA contract and the great adventure of the early 1980s was to deliver it. Peter Bowles, at the height of his popularity after his role in *To the Manor Born,* was brilliantly cast as the often bemused but always well-meaning resident magistrate of the title while Niall Tobin, Brian Murray and the cream of the Irish acting profession supported him. Herbert Wise directed, shooting took place mainly at a rambling country estate near Dublin, and among the many to work on this great project was my younger daughter Sally, hired independently as a 'gofer' by James Mitchell, the producer. A condition of her employment was that she had to drive, and she had to learn fast. An early driving assignment was to ferry the star of the show to and from the location and one Friday evening as she fought her way through the O'Connell Street traffic Bowles inquired in his urbane way: 'I saw an L plate on the back of the car. Who are you teaching to drive?' 'Myself,' replied Sally briskly. Since the fortunes of Ulster Television rested on Bowles, who was insured for a seven-figure sum, it is just as well that Sally was a quick learner. I kept my own visits to the filming to a minimum – it is never good to breathe over a director's shoulder – but when the first series was complete I was almost happy. Amusing and a visual delight, it was what we needed if not what I wanted, and when it went out on Channel 4 in 1983 it found critical and popular acclaim. A second, and better, series followed and a third – they proved equally successful. Thus – albeit after nearly 25 years – Ulster Television had again broken new ground with our first full-blown network drama series. Such undertakings were at the very limit of our capabilities: despite all the acclaim it took a few years before foreign sales finally covered the costs and *The Irish R.M.* was 'in the black'.

For me this was the beginning of a swan song. Ever since we had won the contract battle against NIITV in 1980 I had been conscious that my days as managing director of Ulster Television should come to an end. Though I was still only in my early 50s I was by far the longest-serving chief executive in ITV (as well as the tallest and heaviest, incidentally) and the 'one-man-band' nonsense left me in no doubt that the IBA would prefer to see me 'upstairs' as company chairman. I knew that a new-look management would have to be in place well before the next contract round in the late 1980s. This fitted with my personal feelings since, strangely, I had no desire to go on forever. My decision in the later 1970s to play golf again had given me a fresh taste for other things after the long years of obsessive dedication to the company.

During the contract struggle Pat and I promised ourselves that as soon as the result was known we would have a really good holiday and we picked a destination recommended by my friend and colleague Mike Hutcheson: Naples, Florida. In January 1981, therefore, we checked into the Edgewater Hotel for some winter sun, sea, sand and golf. Naples is a beautiful place on the southwest coast of Florida, close to the Everglades and facing the Gulf of Mexico, and it has been a winter resort for Americans since the likes of Greta Garbo and Gary Cooper took their holidays there. It has everything the visitor could ask for, beaches, good restaurants and shops, and above all (for me at least) it was in easy range of 20 (now 80) golf courses. I was still, at this time, president of the Northern Ireland Chamber of Commerce so I paid a courtesy call on the Naples Chamber and they invited us to join their annual golf event. Even by American standards, which are probably unrivalled, the welcome was warm and the people were friendly; we could hardly have been made to feel more at home. When they heard we were paying for a hotel they quickly pointed out that our money would be much better employed as a deposit on an apartment, or 'condo'. The idea was planted. On return to Belfast we both began to think of a second home in the sun. My mother had left me a modest legacy and this seemed a promising use for it. That autumn we returned to Naples and with the help of our new friends found a 'realtor' to show us properties. Among these was an apartment in a recently-completed building on the edge of a golf course. It didn't quite have a sea view – the sea was just six miles away – but in the contest between gulf and golf the latter had to win.

For personal as well as professional reasons, therefore, I was ready to ease myself out of the Managing Director's seat at Ulster Television. In fact the transition had begun in 1977 after the death of Lord Antrim, when James MacQuitty succeeded as Company Chairman and I moved up to the post of Deputy Chairman, although remaining as Managing Director. In 1983 James reached retiring age so I was to become Chairman. With six years to go before the next contract renewal, this was the moment to appoint my successor. To the Board's surprise I declared that I did not wish to be involved in the selection, since I felt that the new man should have a clear run, with no debts or old loyalties. Unfortunately, things did not work out that way.

The Board appointed a selection panel of three: Arthur Brooke, a retired and brilliant civil servant who had been acting as a consultant to the company, George Cooper, the man who once kept a laminated rate card in his swimming trunks at Cannes and who went on to run first Thames Television and then *TV Times*, and James MacQuitty. The post of Managing Director, Ulster Television, was advertised and the panel reported that the best candidates were outsiders. There were four internal candidates of whom three were long-term colleagues of mine and the fourth was Desmond Smyth, a Queen's University mathematics graduate who had joined us from Price Waterhouse as Chief Accountant in the 1970s and rose to the post of Company Secretary. After long deliberation the panel decided to rule out the internal candidates, although all of them had apparently performed well at interview. The three established figures were near my age and were felt to be insufficiently fresh for the task of leading the company into another contract battle in a few years. Desmond Smyth, on the other hand, was thought to be too young. The spotlight thus fell upon the external applicants. As I heard this reported at a Board meeting my heart sank. I knew that my senior colleagues would be regarded as not from the right generation to take the company forward but what I could not understand was the rejection of Desmond Smyth. Though I had kept silent my expression must have betrayed me for just as the discussion seemed about to end one member remarked: 'Brum doesn't look too happy.' All faces turned towards me and, after some hesitation, I spoke. I said that I felt Desmond Smyth had great promise. Desmond thought clearly and wrote well and had done a fine job in managing the finances of *The Irish R.M.*. Yes, he was young, but not that young - in fact he was 33 and so would be almost 40 by the time the contract came up for renewal - I had to remind the Board that I had been 29 when they gave me the post. Desmond would have the benefit of several years' experience in the company, as well as the back-up of serious administrative, programme and advertising executives who knew the business back to front. Ulster Television would have a well-balanced management team. There followed a brief debate in which these views prevailed, and Desmond was appointed - with the firm proviso that 'Brum must be around'.

It might be said that I was making the very mistake I had sworn to avoid - meddling even before the new management was in place - but that is not how I see it. Reluctantly, I had to act to ensure a sound and promising team to run the company of which I was to be Chairman. I was sincere in my wish to withdraw from day-to-day management and over the next three or four years I tried to visit, rather than inhabit Havelock House and sought to limit my involvement in management. I was spending time with Pat and my daughters, time on the golf course, time in Florida and time on many other matters which had always interested me. Of these last, perhaps the most important was Co-Operation Ireland.

It was in 1979 that I was recruited to this cause by Brendan O'Regan, a distinguished Irishman and a figure of great energy and foresight. His claim to fame was the invention of Duty Free, a novelty he introduced at Shannon Airport and which rapidly spread worldwide. He was chairman of Bord Failte, the Republic's tourist board, and in the late 1970s his fertile mind turned towards Northern Ireland and the question of peace. He foresaw a group called 'Co-Operation North' and came to Havelock House to see me. Politics, he argued, had failed – a difficult view to challenge in those days – and the best hope for the future lay in new approaches based on business, jobs and the young. He knew of my long record of good relations with RTE and of my regard for the South, and he knew too that through the Chamber of Commerce, the Institute of Directors and UTV's unique position in Northern Ireland I was ideally placed to help, so he asked me to join and to recruit like-minded Northerners. It was a meeting of minds. As someone with excellent contacts on both sides of the border I was conscious of the great gulf of misunderstanding which divided the island, while as a businessman I was aware of lost opportunities in many fields of activity. By building understanding and commerce I was sure we could help the cause of peace, and I was equally sure that Brendan O'Regan was the man to lead the way.

So it was that we became partners in what after a few years ceased to be 'Co-Operation North' and became 'Co-Operation Ireland', a unique initiative to foster cross-border contacts and encourage exchanges which would otherwise not have taken place. Looking back, it is difficult to believe how limited these contacts were even 20 years ago. Northern Ireland and the Republic were neighbouring markets with no town more than a few hours from any other and through conferences, projects, awards and a great variety of other schemes we tried to build healthier and more neighbourly relations and also create jobs. Hardship and unemployment had long been recruiting sergeants for the paramilitary groups so we worked for greater prosperity at all levels hoping to reduce the violence. Our efforts helped forge new links in fields such as transport, agriculture and power – for example, I brought together the chiefs of the two electricity boards, North and South. At the same time, Co-Operation Ireland was active with the young, linking schools and clubs North and South, bringing groups of children and young people together and showing them what they had in common. One of our higher-profile events was the 'Maracycle', an annual sponsored cycling event between Dublin and Belfast which proved hugely popular.

All of this required money and finding it was one of my principal jobs. We maintained close and friendly links with government in Dublin, Belfast and London and received some funding from the European Union but our main source of income was the business community in the United States. So it was that I often found myself breaking journeys to and from Florida with a stop-off in New York or Washington or even Los Angeles, where we would visit some captain of industry or attend some business event to pitch for our cause. Brendan would introduce us by saying, 'I am Irish-Irish and Brum is British-Irish.' This usually required further explanation which in turn shed light on what we were about. Once our roles and positions were clear American business people proved receptive to the idea that trade and cultural exchange could promote peace and understanding – sometimes surprisingly receptive. I recall on one occasion visiting a senior executive of Citibank in New York and outside his office I spotted a headline in the *Wall Street Journal* declaring: 'Citibank first half loss $60m; 800 jobs to go.' It seemed a hopeless case but we went in anyway and I opened by saying: 'We know it's probably one of the worst days in your lives here, but we have come to ask you to join our Board and it will only cost you $30,000 a year.' This directness broke the ice and the Citibank man appreciated our honesty so much that – despite the unfortunate timing – he agreed on the spot. Others we recruited included Jack Welsh of General Electric and Roger Smith of General Motors, two of the most powerful businessmen in the world. With the then chairman of American Brands I took an even more ambitious approach. The company owned such firms as Titleist golf balls and White and Mackay whisky, but more relevantly Gallahers cigarettes in Belfast, and I was determined to cash in on this. I explained our usual arrangement for Board membership but then said: 'In your case, however, how about $100,000 for three years, with you becoming chairman?' He chuckled and said: 'Is that all?' To which I answered: 'Well, no. There is the matter of a banquet at the Plaza Hotel which the chairman usually funds.' He agreed with a smile.

Another effort was in the Bahamas where a meeting was arranged by Wilbert Forker, who had been a Methodist minister in Belfast, and so we flew out to Nassau and were whisked off to the Lyford Cay golf club for lunch with the 'prospect'. As we grazed on a rather measly plate of salad leaves Brendan and I made our pitch while 'the prospect' nodded every now and then saying 'very good, very good'. After precisely 40 minutes he got up, said goodbye and walked off. He never contributed.

That visit to the Bahamas was to have unforeseen consequences for my family, and since those events took place in the later 1980s this is a good moment to recount what happened. It all began with a truly remarkable birthday when the Belfast *News Letter*, the oldest English-language newspaper in continuous publication in the world, turned 250 in 1987. Two and a half centuries had passed since Francis Joy printed the first edition in what was then the town of Belfast, and for almost two centuries of that time the paper had been in the care of my family, most recently with Bill as chairman. The birthday was both a moment of history and a moment for celebration, but as preparations went ahead there came a disappointment. Any other newspaper in the United Kingdom, marking a milestone of this kind, could have expected a royal appearance of some sort (when the *Times* reached its 200th birthday, the Queen herself visited the paper), but not the *News Letter*. From 'official' circles the message came that no member of the Royal family, however lowly, could attend. Was this a sign of 'sensitivity' to divided opinion in Northern Ireland? It was certainly poor recompense for the paper's many years of loyalty to the Union and the Crown, not to mention years of dedicated work by so many British subjects. My brother was rightly offended but I suggested that we find a different figurehead for our proceedings and he let me approach an old friend, Lord Deedes. In British newspaper terms, Bill Deedes is the nearest one can get to royalty: the doyen of foreign correspondents whose career stretches back to the 1930s, he was a

Member of Parliament and close adviser to Harold Macmillan before becoming a distinguished editor of the *Daily Telegraph*. In the 1980s he moved on to become a journalist without portfolio for his paper and a figure of great but quiet influence in British life. He and I had met years before in London and enjoyed annual lunches together so I knew of his deep interest in, and sympathy for, Northern Ireland. Now he came to Belfast and graced the celebratory banquet with a magnificent, witty and thoughtful speech. By way of thanks, I gave him a hearty lunch the next day at the Royal County Down, followed by a round of golf which I remember fondly as the best I have ever played (a gross 76 with two doubles on the card).

With the 250th birthday out of the way Bill became reconciled to the view that the Henderson family connection with the paper had to end. Both of us had daughters – he had three to my two – and none of them went into the family business so a new regime was inevitable and it seemed right to sell. The family had long been proud of the paper's independence, for it was rare by then to find a daily or even a weekly which was not part of a large group but it was clear that the *News Letter* might benefit by belonging to something bigger. A merger with the *Belfast Telegraph,* owned by the Thomson organization, was proposed which would have left Bill as chairman. Since both titles were in the same city this was referred to the Monopolies and Mergers Commission. To our disappointment and anger they rejected it. It was at this point that Wilbert Forker entered the frame. When the question of selling the *News Letter* arose he was in touch with me and interested in the outcome, and now, after the MMC ruling, he put together a new group. The terms were much less favourable to the family than the Belfast Telegraph arrangement would have been and Bill could not be given the chair but in time the deal was done. It was a great pity that matters could not have been settled as we had wished but that is business. Most of all it was an enormous wrench for the whole family to break with two and a half centuries of history.

For me there was soon to be another difficult break, this time with Ulster Television. When I moved up from managing director to chairman I envisaged a good 10 years before final retirement, perhaps when I turned 65 in 1994, but this was not to be. I wanted to hand over the daily management and to pursue both my growing interests outside television and the job of chairman. Routinely I backed Desmond Smyth at Board meetings because not only did I have a high opinion of his ability and potential but I also liked him. As the 1980s unfolded, however, some events caused me anxiety. A number of changes in senior management involved displacing experienced people, on a couple of occasions in acrimonious circumstances. I supported these decisions in Board meetings. Against this I saw problems on the programme and advertising sides which I merely mentioned to Desmond privately.

Ever since the days of Lord Hill it had been normal in the ITV companies to complain of the nannying ways of the IBA and the unfairness of the contract system. What other industry, the ITV companies asked, had to put up with such arbitrariness and such periodic upheavals as they went about their legitimate business? How was it fair that a firm with a record of producing decent television and paying good dividends to shareholders could be displaced in favour of an untried rival on the say-so of a collection of amateur do-gooders (the IBA) applying vague, subjective criteria of 'public interest'? To a degree I shared these feelings and I certainly hated the renewal process but I always bore in mind the poet's advice to 'hang on to Nurse, the next may be worse'. In general terms I believed in living with the system and making the best of it. In the course of the 1980s, however, the voices of the complainers rose to become a chorus that Margaret Thatcher's government could not ignore. Now while Thatcher was inclined to do away with the old IBA-style state regulation system she had no intention of letting the ITV companies have things their own way because she had long despised them for their craven attitude towards the trades unions. I had first-hand experience of this when I met her once and she lectured me on the iniquities of restrictive practices in the television industry and the weakness of the managements. I protested that we in the smaller companies were often innocent victims in this and pointed out the Ulster Television had the best productivity figures in the network, to which she replied irritably: 'Oh, I don't mean you, Brum.' As she did in so many other walks of British life Thatcher decided to put the cat among the pigeons: she declared that the contract renewal process of 1990/91 would be a pure auction, with licences going to the highest bidders. There would be no more 'public interest', no more do-gooders, no subjective, behind-the-scenes decision making; it would be a matter of price, full stop. The result of this dramatic decision was a mad panic as the companies suddenly saw that their complaints had got them something *much worse* than they had already: a market where they would have to gamble present cash against future profits and where the advantage lay with the most reckless. A period of ferocious lobbying followed in which – doubtless to Thatcher's amusement – the principled opponents of 'public interest' criteria performed a complete about-face and began to argue that such an important matter as an ITV licence could not be decided on money grounds alone. In the end a hybrid system was introduced but, for the first time, money 'up front' was the principal part of the process.

Inevitably as an ITV company chairman I was involved in all this politicking, but as the arguments in London ebbed and flowed I was worried by more than the money question. In 1980 I had run the operation to defeat NIITV not so much like a military campaign as like a total war, ensuring that all our biggest battalions – Gloria Hunniford, *The Irish R.M.*, our record in the Troubles, even my leading roles in the Chamber of Commerce and the Royal Television Society – were deployed to the best possible advantage from start to finish. I knew the commitment required and I knew the stakes. I also knew the history: Ulster Television had survived every renewal to date while a dozen companies had lost their licences; we were now defying the odds and so we needed to try even harder with each new round. Even from Florida I saw a danger of over-confidence. Some directors and many staff who wrote or spoke to me (although I always discouraged such contacts) confirmed this view. Worse still, it was soon clear that there would be two other bidders for the Northern Ireland licence and each of them presented a formidable challenge. First came TVNi, whose leading lights were Roy Bailie, a prominent businessman, and the talented Alan Wright, who had been a producer on *Good Evening Ulster* before going on to work at RTE and in the independent sector. They were advised by Tony Fleck, previously the IBA's man in Belfast. The highlights of their bid would be a chain of one-off network dramas, a locally-based soap opera and more extensive outside broadcast work. The other group was Lagan Television, headed by another leading local businessman, Dawson Moreland, and backed by, among others, Barney Eastwood, Robert McCartney and Phil Coulter. Their proposed chief executive was a heavyweight, the former controller of BBC1 and former boss of Thames Television Bryan Cowgill, supported by a former BBC producer, Chris Parr.

Ulster Television's financial position at this time was roughly as follows. We were turning a profit of over £2m, mainly accounted for by our very favourable deal on revenue from Channel 4, which amounted to just that sum: £2m. Unfortunately that deal was about to expire and the annual £2m would disappear with it, so in effect the company was in balance and no more – hardly a good basis for drawing up grand new investment plans with which to delight the IBA, or indeed for tabling a large cash bid. I did not regard the battle as lost and offered to Desmond a local programme production plan of ruthless realism in our bid. We would still have good programmes, for example the latest version of the evening magazine, which still outstripped the local BBC's alternative, and Gerry Kelly's Friday evening show, which was a reliable audience-winner. Beyond these and a few others, my suggestion was to cut our cloth as tightly as possible. This 'siege' plan was approved by Desmond and the Board. I argued that we should present ourselves to the IBA as the experienced, prudent players who knew what could be done and what could not. We could offer blood, toil, sweat and tears through these straitened times, with firm promises of expansion of ideas when conditions truly allowed – a strong contrast to the blithe optimism and grand promises of our rivals.

It was on the question of a cash bid that divisions arose. I had learned, confidentially, that TVNi were bidding £2m for the contract and Lagan £3m, both far too high considering the outlook for advertising revenue in Northern Ireland at the time. I was also aware, because the government had said so, that money alone would not decide the result and that public interest was still important. My view was this: we were the only company among the three bidders which was actually doing this job and our results and experienced forecasts indicated that the business would not yield large profits in the short or medium term, indeed it might not yield any profit at all. On that basis no responsible company could bid millions of pounds for the licence. In fact, I felt that we should bid a token £5,000 and make a virtue of it, holding it up as proof that we were prudent and reliable businessmen. I was encouraged in this view by a private tip-off that Scottish Television was adopting a similar stance.

I was in Florida when news reached me that Desmond and certain Board members had been speaking about management concern at my approach and were canvassing the idea of a £1m bid. I could scarcely believe this for it seemed the worst of all worlds. At a stroke we would achieve three things: we would plunge the company into the red on existing budgets; we would destroy our standing as the prudent and experienced player in the contest and we would still be the lowest bidder in the auction. The £1m bid, in short, knocked all the logic out of our position. Yet on my return to Belfast I found that roughly half the Board had been won over to Desmond's position. They did not know, as I did, that Scottish planned a similar strategy and for reasons of confidentiality I was not free to tell them. On the other hand many of them I had regarded as friends and they had all been well treated over the years – I might have been able to count on their trust. As Chairman I now found myself in a most unpleasant position: I could challenge Desmond, split the Board and fight the battle or I could bow out and let him do it his way, even though I felt strongly that his way was unwise. After painful reflection I chose the latter course and resigned as Chairman and soon afterwards from the Board. My departure from Ulster Television was dated November

1990, 32 years and a couple of months after I received that phone call from Paddy Falloon that drew me into the business. I was 61.

Two footnotes here – the first is that my departure was marked by some gracelessness on the part of the company and the second is that they won the contest for the licence. The latter is not proof that the £1m bid was justified; Scottish Television won theirs with a bid of £10,000 and Ulster Television could have done the same. In the event a rising advertising tide saved the company.

14
Never a Dull Moment

There was never any danger of idleness after Ulster Television. Certainly there is always reflection, but I immediately sought to savour and recover some of the loves of my life. Our home is in the County Down hills near Ballynahinch within easy reach of many friends and of Royal County Down and Malone golf courses. On gardening it is Pat who has the horticultural vision and it is she who plants all those delicate shoots with polysyllabic Latin names; mine is the intrusive hoe, shears and clippers which occasionally (too frequently, alas) mistake an exotic plant for a weed and healthy growth for unwanted sprawl. So, it is trimming bushes and trees, pulling out brambles and ivy and dead-heading rhododendrons - 10 thousand a year! Satisfying and good for the health although to the outsider the results are invisible. In the colder, greyer months when the garden is dormant we spend a good deal of time in Florida, where there are also good friends and good bridge and golf. My daughters, Glynis and Sally, continue to bring me great joy and pride and since 13th July 1999 I have a grandson, William - Sally's boy - who brings new delights.

There are other pleasures and tasks. Until 2001 I was involved at Queen's University as a member of the Senate and on my retirement from it they kindly awarded me an honorary degree. I also continued my passion for theatre through the Association of Ulster Drama Festivals, mentioned in earlier chapters, having become its president in 1984 on the death of Lady Antrim. There was little for me to do since the operation was run so well by the excellent Beth Duffin but I was consulted on major decisions and saw at first hand the emergence of some first-class acting and directing talent. Every year the best of the festival winners have the chance to perform in the finals which are both a cultural and a social event. Although it was

IRA bombs which forced us to switch the venue from the Grand Opera House to the Lyric Theatre, my view was that this was an improvement. On relinquishing the presidency to my friend Rowel Friers it was tragic that he died soon afterwards and I returned to the post for a period until his successor was found – a fine lady in Rosemary Kelly, albeit from the BBC!

A more ambitious sideline came my way for much of the 1990s. This was Laganside, a body created to promote the rejuvenation of Belfast's waterfront, at the invitation of Richard Needham, an ebullient and energetic minister at the Northern Ireland Office. The board was fairly amateur in these matters, but was enthusiastically led by the Duke of Abercorn, who had Needham's support. We set about the multi-million-pound, 10-year task of transforming the Lagan banks into a vibrant 21st century complex of office buildings, apartments, houses and hotels. It was sad when the Liverpool and Heysham steamers moved downriver and their red and yellow funnels ceased to be a familiar sight in city-centre Belfast, but on the other hand few mourned the loss of those grim stacks of coal and rusting iron on the east bank. These were replaced in due course by something else in which I had a hand, Belfast's principal Millennium project. This was the proposal – backed by the Sports, Arts and Youth Councils and the Ulster Museum – to create a splendid 12,000-seater arena and dome, flanked by Arts and Sciences Centres on this site near the city's heart. Brian Musgrave, seconded from the Department of the Environment, and I prepared the bid for £100m from the National Millennium Commission. The project hit a rocky patch and seemed doomed to be watered down, and Brian and I moved on, but not long afterwards the government found fresh funds and our ideas were revived. In consequence Belfast gained a huge new entertainment venue combined with fine cultural amenities for the public at large – and especially for the young. There can surely be few people who know the city well who would dispute that the transformation of the once-grim Lagan banks have been an enormous boon for Belfast, its people and its standing in the world.

Another absorbing commitment, and one which in some ways grew out of the Laganside experience, was the Ulster Waterways Group which I started in 1993. This impressive and effective body has the mission of reopening the network of rivers and canals which once served the province. The cost of this enterprise, in 1997 prices, is an estimated £120m, which seems to me a remarkably modest sum, particularly when spread over the 10 years or more that it would take to complete. We have made a start and the benefits, in terms of quality of life, leisure and, not least, jobs, are considerable, while the work is also valuable for North-South co-operation. If this sounds like a sales pitch (and it is one I have made many times), it is heartfelt. The slow pace and the canal routes give a different and often a better perspective on the world. Belfast to Limerick by water my slogan.

One more task has absorbed and pleased me in the course of a retirement that has been far busier than I ever intended. In 1996 I first heard people talking about how my local town might mark the bicentenary of the '98', in which it played a very special part. Ulster's role in the great and tragic rebellion of 1798 came to its gory end in the battle of Ballynahinch one sunny morning in June of that year when the soldiers of General Nugent over-ran the ill-disciplined rebel force led by Henry Munro. Elizabeth 'Betsy' Gray of Gransha, a rebel messenger, was shot alongside her brother and her lover once the dragoons had cleared the town and she has been a local heroine ever since, by far the best-remembered character in the whole drama. In our more recent Troubles Ballynahinch has been relatively peaceful, but in 1996 I believed that this anniversary would be wide open to abuse by extremists of all sorts and decided to do what I could to prevent that and ensure that it was marked in a way which did lasting credit to the town.

The truth about the rebellion in County Down is complex and sad and any political resonance that people claim to detect in it today is probably false. The cause may have been a 'green' one in the sense that the aim of the rising was to secure Irish independence, but it was not anti-Protestant. In fact the rebel force at Ballynahinch was largely Protestant drawn from the dissenting, Presbyterian population, who even more than Ireland's Catholics, had long been victims of discrimination and unfair tenancy laws (it was this which had prompted many members of that community to emigrate to America, a good number of them going on to figure among the founding revolutionary fathers of the United States). To add to the religious confusion of the time, General Nugent's army included many Catholics. Moreover, the rebels were not religious bigots and nor did they hate the English; on the contrary, they were explicitly sworn to tolerance and were inspired by the best ideals of the American and French Revolutions. There is much to admire, even if the story of the rising shows it to have been naive and sometimes pathetic – the poorly-armed rebel soldiers, for example, wore their Sunday best for the campaign, and Munro ruled out a night attack on Nugent's army on the grounds that such tactics would be underhand.

I thought that we must not allow these events to be exploited for propaganda. I found support from an old friend, Neil Shawcross, a distinguished artist who had tutored my daughter Sally, and from a local insurance broker, Brendan Maguire (son of a former BBC Controller in Northern Ireland, Waldo Maguire). I also chanced upon a wonderful local historian in the form of Horace Reid, who provided the essential facts for our endeavours. We marked the anniversary by installing four large outdoor murals in prominent positions in the town, all depicting moments and scenes from the history of Ballynahinch and notably from the battle. The inspiration for this came from a visit I had made in 1995 to the town of Chemaimus in British Columbia. Chemaimus had been an industrial centre with coal, steel and timber industries but when these faded it set about transforming itself into a cultural and tourist attraction. Far from concealing their past, the townspeople commemorated their old trades in big, dramatic murals – an exciting and successful device. Ballynahinch has problems of its own; once a prosperous market town it has suffered from the competition of supermarkets and from the commuter-belt mentality and is seen by many as little more than an irritating traffic bottleneck. Serious efforts are being made to change this and revive the town centre and once the 1998 anniversary was out of the way (without any increase in local tension, I am glad to say) I felt the murals should become a long-term project which might give an added dimension to this regeneration. I had paid for the first four myself – they were painted by Bill Gatt and Ian Morrow – but now threw myself into the business of raising money for more. Thanks to general enthusiasm and generosity, by the year 2000 we had 12 murals and a plan for a total of 30, painted by a variety of local artists. Hundreds of people are involved, and of course tens of thousands see the murals and, I hope, derive some pleasure and education from them. The regeneration movement in the town continues under the visionary Vincent Fullam who, with the team he leads, gives us all hope that the cameraderie and energy will bring a diversity of benefit to all.

This book has itself provided me with another significant occupation in recent years, and as I dictate these words I am aware that that particular task is drawing to its close. On my 70th birthday we had a party at the Culloden Hotel for lots of our relations and friends, drawn from far and near and from the recent and the distant past. It is a fine venue and one I know well – for years I have been a regular member of the Culloden's 'chain gang', the bevy of after-dinner speakers who wore some form of ceremonial chain as president of this or chairman of that. With Pat and Glynis close by me (Sally was at her London home with the new-born William), I shared memories and saw faces from almost every year of a life blessed in many, many ways.

Looking back over those years and reading over the chapters of this narrative it strikes me that the story seems to have some coherence, although never at any point could I be said to have planned it. A few distinct themes recur, as if they were strands of cloth woven together into a single strong belt or rope. Perhaps a love of history? That surfaces again and again, from my Trinity days through the historical programmes at UTV to the Ballynahinch murals. Even when its role has not been obvious it has influenced me – any perspective I had on the Troubles, for one, owes a good deal to my respect for the past. Another obvious theme was drama; I adored the stage and still do and that passion pushed me into television. No doubt, too, it helps account for my taste for public speaking. A third theme, perhaps even more important, is a never-ending desire for good fellowship. From those hedonistic days in Trinity, when the rooms in Front Square that I shared with Randal Kinkead were the setting for a continual round of parties, through the Natural Break golf weekends to that 70th birthday celebration, I have always loved a good time. Yes, I like the laughter, stories and release of tension and I also relish and treasure the feeling of bringing people together. Whether it was lunching and playing golf with advertising agents, sharing a Friday evening drink with trade union shop stewards or pressing the cause of Co-Operation Ireland, I have always felt that by sharing the enjoyment of life people learn to understand one another better. I am restless and have a drive to push that process onward and help people enjoy each other's company. This, no doubt, is one reason why I dedicated so much of my life to the 'fun factory' of television.

The strongest theme of all, though I keep well concealed, is my love of family and sense of family heritage. For centuries the Hendersons were good business people, enterprising newspapermen and proud citizens of Belfast, and they had a strong sense of loyalty towards this perplexing and fascinating land.

I was enormously fortunate in finding my niche so early in life and in having 30 years at the top in independent television. To have helped build Ulster Television and place it at the heart of Northern Ireland life, to have played a part in ITV nationally, to have met and worked with so many brilliant and remarkable people and, above all, to have had the chance to test my own abilities to the limit, was always a surprise but is of enormous satisfaction. It was never easy, in fact it was pretty hard work. I am most grateful for what came my way. Those long hours were an important cause of the breakdown of my first marriage and I am still conscious of that but I have been the luckiest of men in finding Pat. She, my daughters and my grandson are my loves and my pride. And with that final mention of the four people closest to my heart, it is the place to put my full stop.

before b... g
He became Chairman of U.T.V in 1984 and retire
ul Ulster Waterways, the redevelopment of Belfast's Laganside and the launch
a past President of the Northern Ireland Chamber of Commerce and Industry an
theatre, cinema and golf and is an enthusiastic member of the Royal County Dow
included Midnight Oil (1961); A Television First (1977); A Musing – on th
yal County Down – The First 100 Years (1989). Brumwell Henderson C.B.E
blin, and spent the early years of his career in newspaper journalism before becomin
3. He became Chairman of U.T.V in 1984 and retired in 1990. He has been activel
evelopment of Belfast's Laganside and the launch of celebratory historic murals
ern Ireland Chamber of Commerce and Industry and President of the Associatio
is an enthusiastic member of the Royal County Down Golf Club and Royal Pal
; A Television First (1977); A Musing – on the lighter side of Ulster Televiso
irst 100 Years (1989). Brumwell Henderson C.B.E., M.A., D.Litt., F.R.T.S
s of his career in newspaper journalism before becoming Ulster Television's (U.T.V
TV in 1984 and retired in 1990. He has been actively involved in projects as divers
and the launch of celebratory historic murals in Ballynahinch, Co. Down. He ha
e and Industry and President of the Association of Ulster Drama Festivals. Fo
Royal County Down Golf Club and Royal Palm Golf Club, Naples, Florida. H
Musing – on the lighter side of Ulster Televison and its first 25 years (1984); an
ell Henderson C.B.E., M.A., D.Litt., F.R.T.S., F.Inst.D., F.C.I.M., wa
ournalism before becoming Ulster Television's (U.T.V) first Managing Director
1990. He has been actively involved in projects as diverse as Co-Operation Irelan
ory historic murals in Ballynahinch, Co. Down. He has been, among other thing
nt of the Association of Ulster Drama Festivals. For recreation, he enjoys readin
Club and Royal Palm Golf Club, Naples, Florida. His previous publications hav
side of Ulster Televison and its first 25 years (1984); and (with Harry McCaw
A., D.Litt., F.R.T.S., F.Inst.D., F.C.I.M., was educated at Trinity Colleg
lster Television's (U.T.V) first Managing Director, a position he held from 1959 t
involved in projects as diverse as Co-Operation Ireland and Ulster Waterways, th
llynahinch, Co. Down. He has been, among other things, a past President of th
of Ulster Drama Festivals. For recreation, he enjoys reading, theatre, cinema an
lm Golf Club, Naples, Florida. His previous publications have included Midnigh
on and its first 25 years (1984); and (with Harry McCaw) Royal County Dow
S., F.Inst.D., F.C.I.M., was educated at Trinity College, Dublin, and spent th
TV) first Managing Director, a position he held from 1959 to 1983. He becam
as diverse as Co-Operation Ireland and Ulster Waterways, the redevelopment
own. He has been, among other things, a past President of the Northern Irelan
a Festivals. For recreation, he enjoys reading, theatre, cinema and golf and is a
Naples, Florida. His previous publications have included Midnight Oil (1961); A
25 years (1984); and (with Harry McCaw) Royal County Down – The Firs
F.R.T.S., F.Inst.D., F.C.I.M., was educated at Trinity College, Dublin, an
newspaper journalism before becoming Ulster Television's (U.T.V) firs
... from 1959 to 1983. He became Chairma

runwell Henderson C.
I.A., D.Litt., F.R.T.S., F.Inst.D., F.C.I.M., was educat
rinity College, Dublin, and spent the early years of his career in newspaper jou
lster Television's (UTV) first Managing Director, a position he held from 1959 t
1990. He has been actively involved in projects as diverse as Co-Operation Ire
lebratory historic murals in Ballynahinch, Co. Down. He has been, among other t
resident of the Association of Ulster Drama Festivals. For recreation, he enjoys r
lf Club and Royal Palm Golf Club, Naples, Florida. His previous publications
hter side of Ulster Televison and its first 25 years (1984); and (with Harry McCa
I.A., D.Litt., F.R.T.S., F.Inst.D., F.C.I.M., was educated at Trinity Colleg
lster Television's (UTV) first Managing Director, a position he held from 1959 t
volved in projects as diverse as Co-Operation Ireland and Ulster Waterways, t
allynahinch, Co. Down. He has been, among other things, a past President of the
Ulster Drama Festivals. For recreation, he enjoys reading, theatre, cinema and g
lf Club, Naples, Florida. His previous publications have included Midnight Oil (
d its first 25 years (1984); and (with Harry McCaw) Royal County Down – T
Inst.D., F.C.I.M., was educated at Trinity College, Dublin, and spent the ear
st Managing Director, a position he held from 1959 to 1983. He became Chairma
Co-Operation Ireland and Ulster Waterways, the redevelopment of Belfast's La
en, among other things, a past President of the Northern Ireland Chamber of Co
creation, he enjoys reading, theatre, cinema and golf and is an enthusiastic member o
evious publications have included Midnight Oil (1961); A Television First (197
ith Harry McCaw) Royal County Down – The First 100 Years (1989). B
ucated at Trinity College, Dublin, and spent the early years of his career in newsp
sition he held from 1959 to 1983. He became Chairman of UTV in 1984 and reti
d Ulster Waterways, the redevelopment of Belfast's Laganside and the launch of c
past President of the Northern Ireland Chamber of Commerce and Industry and P
eatre, cinema and golf and is an enthusiastic member of the Royal County Down
luded Midnight Oil (1961); A Television First (1977); A Musing – on the l
oyal County Down – The First 100 Years (1989). Brumwell Henderson C.B.
ublin, and spent the early years of his career in newspaper journalism before becom
83. He became Chairman of UTV in 1984 and retired in 1990. He has been act
development of Belfast's Laganside and the launch of celebratory historic murals
orthern Ireland Chamber of Commerce and Industry and President of the Asso
lf and is an enthusiastic member of the Royal County Down Golf Club and Ro
il (1961); A Television First (1977); A Musing – on the lighter side of Ulster
The First 100 Years (1989). Brumwell Henderson C.B.E., M.A., D.Litt., F
rly years of his career in newspaper journalism before becoming Ulster Televisio
hairman of UTV in 1984 and retired in 1990. He has been actively involved in p
elfast's Laganside and the launch of celebratory historic murals in Ballynahinch,
hamber of Commerce and Industry and President of the Association of Ulster
thusiastic member of the Royal County Down Golf Club and Royal Palm Golf
First (1977); A Musing – on the lighter side of Ulster Televison and i
Brumwell Henderson C.B.E., M.A., D